THE BIBLE

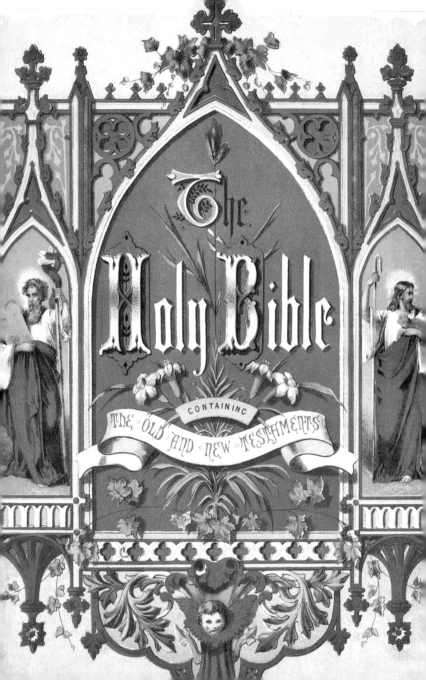

The Holy Bible

CONTAINING

THE OLD AND NEW TESTAMENTS

THE BIBLE

·

John Riches

A BRIEF INSIGHT

STERLING

New York / London
www.sterlingpublishing.com

Library of Congress Cataloging-in-Publication Data
Riches, John Kenneth.
  The Bible : a brief insight / John Riches. -- Illustrated ed.
    p. cm.
  Includes bibliographical references (p.   ) and indexes.
  ISBN 978-1-4027-7536-9
  1. Bible--Introductions. 2. Bible--Use. I. Title.
  BS445.R52 2010
  220.6'1--dc22
                                                    2010008013

10 9 8 7 6 5 4 3 2 1

Published by Sterling Publishing Co., Inc.
387 Park Avenue South, New York, NY 10016

Published by arrangement with Oxford University Press, Inc.

© 2000 by John Riches
Illustrated edition published in 2010 by Sterling Publishing Co., Inc.
Additional text © 2010 Sterling Publishing Co., Inc.

Distributed in Canada by Sterling Publishing
c/o Canadian Manda Group, 165 Dufferin Street
Toronto, Ontario, Canada M6K 3H6

Book design: Faceout Studio

Grateful acknowledgment is made to Jewish Lights Publishing (P.O. Box 237, Woodstock, VT 05091
www.jewishlights.com) for permission to reprint excerpts from *The Last Trial: On the Legends and
Lore of the Command to Abraham to Offer Isaac as a Sacrifice* by Shalom Spiegel, translated and with an
introduction by Judah Goldin.

Please see picture credits on page 223 for image copyright information.

Sterling ISBN 978-1-4027-7536-9

For information about custom editions, special sales, premium and corporate purchases, please contact
Sterling Special Sales Department at 800-805-5489 or specialsales@sterlingpublishing.com.

Frontispiece: This stately frontispiece comes from a ca. 1880 edition of *Brown's Self-Interpreting Bible*,
first published in 1778. The popular tome was the work of Scottish theologian John Brown (1722–87).

CONTENTS

•

ONE

The Bible in the Modern World: Classic or Sacred Text?

●

IT IS SOMETIMES SAID that there are more unread copies of the Bible than of any other book in the world. Such a claim is difficult to prove, though it clearly reflects widespread concern among Christians in Europe about growing levels of ignorance of the Bible's contents. However, it also misses an arguably more significant truth, namely that the Bible is still one of the most influential and widely read books in the world.

It would be interesting to run a competition to find out Today's Most Influential Book and Today's Most Read Book in the World—not by any means the same thing. Marx's *Das Kapital* might until recently

A man in Lalibela, Ethiopia, holds a Bible printed in his native language. The Bible was first translated into Ge'ez (Ethiopic) by Syrian monks. The Ethiopian Bible contains a number of books considered apocryphal in the West, including the Book of Enoch, the full text of which is available only in Ethiopic.

have qualified for the first, though hardly for the second; Thomas Paine's *The Rights of Man* and Adam Smith's *The Wealth of Nations* might get short-listed for the first too. There would surely be candidates of this kind from the sciences (such as Darwin's *Origin of Species*), and from philosophy, literature, and the arts. How would they fare in relation to the great central texts of the major world faiths? "Influence" is not too precise a measure and the eventual outcome of such a competition would probably say as much about the judges as about the winner.

The list of leading contenders for Today's Most Read Book in the World would feature some literary classics and some favorite children's books, though these would probably be surpassed by works of light romantic fiction and crime novels. Popular though these titles are, their appeal tends to be limited to a particular culture. By contrast, the principal religious texts of the major world faiths, with their regular use in worship and private devotion, and their role in the spiritual formation of the adherents and officials of widely dispersed communities, attain a much wider readership.

From time to time certain political texts may emerge to challenge the position of works such as the Koran and the Bible at or near the top of both lists. Chairman Mao's Little Red Book must in its day have had a huge readership and exercised a profound influence over the people of China. But such supremacy was short-lived. The major religious texts have the greater staying power.

The point of this imaginary competition is not to claim any particular moral or aesthetic superiority for any particular text. That would have to be argued on quite different grounds, if it could be argued at all. The point is to show up, right from the beginning, something of the very special quality of such major religious texts. They are immensely influential over people's lives and are read by people of vastly different educational and cultural backgrounds. How do they do it?

It is not my task to answer that question for the Koran, though it would be very interesting to consider what these two texts, or collections of texts, have in common. It is, however, the major purpose of this *Very Short Introduction* to answer it for the Bible. Why does this ancient collection of texts continue to exercise such power over people's lives in our modern, postcolonial, postindustrial world?

Let me first however introduce some of today's Bible readers, simply to communicate something of its extraordinary appeal, its

The nineteenth century saw a huge expansion in the numbers of Bibles in circulation throughout the world. The organization known as Gideons International, founded in 1899, has worked tirelessly to ensure that the Bible is available in hotel rooms and other meeting places. This stack of Gideon Bibles was photographed in 1913.

BEST-SELLING TITLES WORLDWIDE

Bible: 2.5 billion between 1815 and 1975; 20,751,515 distributed in 1998.

Bible, translations of: At least part of the Bible is available in 2,212 of the world's 6,500 languages. The whole Bible is translated into over 350 languages.

Best-selling titles: The world's best-selling copyright book is *The Guinness Book of Records*, with sales of 80 million (1955–97).

Best-selling author: Agatha Christie, whose 78 crime novels have sold ca. 2 billion copies.

Best-selling novels: *Gone with the Wind* (1936), *To Kill a Mockingbird* (1960), and *Valley of the Dolls* (1966) are all said to have sold over 30 million copies.

ability to speak, negatively or positively, to people of different education, culture, and beliefs; but also to portray something of the great diversity of readings which are made of it.

Renee Zulu is part of a remarkable group of women in Soweto, Johannesburg's major black township. This group, the Zamani Soweto Sisters, emerged out of the deep trauma of the 1976 Soweto uprisings, when many young people were killed by the South African police, and is active in community education and development. The Sisters became a powerful educational force, training women in literacy, sewing, dressmaking, household management, even bricklaying. They made beautiful patchwork quilts, which they exhibited in Glasgow in 1983, and smaller collages, following an idea from Chilean refugees, in which they portrayed the struggles, traumas, and hopes of their lives in Soweto.

Renee is an avid Bible reader. She belongs to one of the African Independent Churches, which has its roots in Zimbabwe. Once a year for two weeks, she goes with members of her church to spend time in prayer, singing, and Bible study. The rich narratives and poetry of the Bible provide her with a source of strength, comfort, and delight in a life otherwise marked by hard, repetitive work and economic and political struggle.

Sister Mary John Mananzan of the Philippines, seen in this 2005 photograph, ties white ribbon around a railing in Manila during a demonstration in which participants demanded the resignation of Philippine president Gloria Arroyo. Sr. Mary John's fearless quest for justice is deeply rooted in her readings of the Bible.

Mary John Mananzan is a Benedictine sister from the Philippines, who is also chairperson of Gabriela, a women's organization with 40,000 members from grassroots organizations. This involvement in the struggle for women's dignity and rights led her to question the type of devotion to Mary which was prevalent. Filipina women were encouraged to be submissive and obedient to their husbands and superiors, as Mary was submissive to God's purposes in agreeing to bear his son: "be it unto me according to thy word." Mary John found ammunition against such kinds of Marian piety in Mary's Hymn of praise in Luke's Gospel, known in the church as the Magnificat. In it she sings of her God:

> He has shown strength with his arm,
> he has scattered the proud in the imagination of their hearts,
> he has put down the mighty from their thrones,
> and exalted those of low degree;
> he has filled the hungry with good things,
> and the rich he has sent empty away.

Luke 1:46–55

Here was a vision of a Mary altogether more active and subversive, who worships a God who supports the poor and dispossesses the wealthy. Mary John took the students in her classes on demonstrations. "Teaching social action not social graces" was how an article in the *New York Herald Tribune* described it.

Bishop Dinis Singulane is an Anglican bishop in Mozambique. For years after independence the country was racked by a terrible civil war between RENAMO and FRELIMO. Bishop Dinis was part of a church group involved in the peace process. At one crucial meeting with the

RENAMO leader, he took out his Bible and read two verses from the Sermon on the Mount (Matthew 5:7, 9):

> Blessed are the merciful, for they shall obtain mercy.
> Blessed are the peacemakers, for they shall be called sons of God.

He pleaded with the leader to have mercy on the people of Mozambique and to stop the fighting. He appealed to him to become a peacemaker, for then he would be called a son of God. "If however you choose not to work for peace," continued the bishop, "then we shall want to know whose son you are." The leader asked Bishop Dinis to leave his Bible behind so that he could use it with his generals.

Daniel Boyarin is an Orthodox Jew who teaches Rabbinic Studies in California. For some time he taught at Bar-Ilan University in Jerusalem. In his book *A Radical Jew: Paul and the Politics of Identity*, he argues that Paul, precisely as a Jew, was profoundly critical of those tendencies in the tradition which emphasized Jewish difference and particularity. "There is neither Jew nor Greek, there is neither slave nor free, there is neither male nor female; for you are all one in Christ Jesus" (Galatians 3:28).

Such universalizing tendencies are not, however, without their dangers. What about those who wish to hold on to the old distinctions? What place is there for them in this brave new world? The subsequent history of Jewish-Christian relations shows how terrible the consequences of this refusal to recognize the particular identity of the Jews have been. But equally, Jewish desire to restore and maintain their particular attachments to the Land of Israel has brought its own severe problems. Boyarin's view is that Jewish existence in the Diaspora (that is to say, in Jewish communities outside Israel) is a better model for intercommunity relations than

This photograph of Tim LaHaye, coauthor with Jerry B. Jenkins of the Left Behind series of Christian apocalyptic fiction, was taken at a book signing for his novel *Glorious Appearing* during a 2004 publicity tour.

the Zionist vision of restoration. Paul's cultural critique of Judaism has to be heard, just as it too has to be subjected to radical critique.

One last example of a Bible reader less attractive to liberal sentiment. In his fascinating travel narrative *The Divine Supermarket*, Malise Ruthven describes a meeting with the Reverend Tim LaHaye, one of the leading proponents of so-called Armageddon theology—someone, that is, who believes that the Bible has revealed a precise scenario for the end of the world. It starts with the establishment of the State of Israel, includes the restoration of the Temple, a massive world war, the conversion of the Jews, and the transporting of true believers into heaven ("the rapture").

"The Bible says, 'No man knows the day or the hour,'" said LaHaye. "But we can know the season. . . . One of the most important signs is that Israel and Russia are both dominant players on the world scene, just as the prophets said they would be 2,500 years ago. Russia was just a nothing power till our generation, and Israel was not even in the land." He went on to quote a passage from Ezekiel about the invasion of Israel from the north. God, he believed, would supernaturally intervene to destroy Russia in the midst of its attack on Israel.

One could go on. It is perhaps appropriate to end with someone like LaHaye, lest this more or less random and personal list of Bible readers should seem too apologetic or optimistic. It is not any part of my purpose to present a bland or anodyne view of the Bible. I am fully aware that the Bible has been used for purposes which for many are profoundly abhorrent, as well as in the cause of justice and liberation. It is true, for instance, that many members of the Dutch Reformed Churches, which supported apartheid, sincerely believed that such policies were biblical and therefore theologically justified. At the same time, I am also aware of those engaged in the struggle against apartheid for whom the Bible was a source of moral and religious guidance and enlightenment. The fact that we have to contend with is that both sides could appeal to the Bible for enlightenment and guidance. The sheer diversity of the ways in which the Bible has been embodied in Jewish and Christian communities is both fascinating and disturbing.

One task of this book will be to look at the way the Bible was formed, to see what clues this might offer to the reasons for this bewildering diversity of interpretations. Chapter 2 looks at some of the processes of tradition and composition that led to the final form of the biblical books as we know them today. In Chapter 3 we will look at the process whereby different books came to be included in the various Bibles which are now accepted as authoritative (canonical) in various religious communities, Jewish and Christian.

The rest of the book will focus more on the different kinds of readings which the Bible has received in its long history. We shall look, in Chapter 4, at some of the readings of the Bible by believers, both Jews and Christians. Chapter 5 concentrates on critical readings, mainly from the Reformation and the Enlightenment, which had radical effects on how the Bible was perceived. This will be followed, in Chapter 6, by discussions of the ways the Bible has been received outside the traditional homelands of Christianity. Chapter 7 looks at the part that the Bible has played in high and popular culture. Chapter 8 discusses its place in the world of politics and a summary concludes the book in Chapter 9.

The relationship between readers and text is, of course, a very complex one. Is it the diversity of the Bible which creates such a wide array of communities of readers? Or do different readers shape the Bible to their own ends and purposes, either literally, by deciding which books should or should not be included, or figuratively, by the different reading strategies which they adopt? This issue will accompany us through the book, as we investigate the various ways in which the Bible has been read and lived out.

At this point I should enter a strong disclaimer. I cannot possibly speak for all readers of the Bible, or even give a fair selection of different points of view about the Bible. For a start, as Chapter 3 illustrates, there is no such thing as "the Bible": there are a significant number of Bibles, which differ both in the books included and in the order in which those books occur. In the second place, the Bible belongs to a wide range of religious (and not so religious) communities the world over. I am a white, male, European, English-born, Anglican Christian teaching New Testament in a Scottish university. Universities are, in intention at least, open-minded places, where a certain internationalism is fostered. We have been fortunate in the stream of overseas students and visitors who have enriched our collegiate life. But while all of this helps to enlarge one's sense of who one is, I cannot pretend that it enables me wholly to transcend the social and cultural mix that, in part at least, makes me who I am. I belong to a particular community of readers, albeit one which has links with other such communities. But we can only do our reading and thinking within our own particular context, facing the questions which are of particular urgency for us, reflecting the kinds of deep-seated beliefs and assumptions which are ours. Of course, some of the questions which concern me from my perspective will be global questions, of concern to many communities around the world. Even so, I will inevitably reflect on such questions from my perspective. I will try to be as open as I can about such slants, but readers should beware!

ΤΗΝ ΙΔΙΑΝ ΑΥΤΩΝ ΑΠΩΛΕΙΑΝ
ΜΕΙС ΟΥΝ ΑΓΑΠΗΤΟΙ ΠΡΟΓΙ̅Ω
СКОΝΤΕС ΦΥΛΑССΕСΘΕ
ΙΝΑ ΜΗ ΤΗ ΤΩΝ ΑΘΕСΜΩΝ ΠΛΑ
ΝΗ СΥΝΑΠΑΧΘΕΝΤΕС ΕΚΠΕ
СΗ ΤΕ ΤΟΥ ΙΔΙΟΥ СΤΗΡΙΓΜΟΥ
ΑΥΞΑΝΕΤΕ ΔΕ ΕΝ ΧΑΡΙΤΙ ΚΑΙ ΓΝΩ
СΕΙ ΤΟΥ Κ̅Υ̅ ΗΜΩΝ ΚΑΙ С̅Ρ̅С̅ Ι̅Υ̅ Χ̅Υ̅
ΑΥΤΩ Η ΔΟΞΑ ΚΑΙ ΝΥΝ ΚΑΙ ΕΙС
ΗΜΕΡΑΝ ΑΙΩΝΟС ΑΜΗΝ

ΠΕΤΡΟΥ

ΙΩΑΝΝΟΥ

ΗΝ ΑΠ ΑΡΧΗС Ο ΑΚΗΚΟΑΜΕΝ Ο ΕΩΡΑ
ΚΑΜΕΝ ΤΟΙС ΟΦΘΑΛΜΟΙС ΗΜΩ
Ο ΕΘΕΑСΑΜΕΘΑ ΚΑΙ ΑΙ ΧΕΙΡΕС ΗΜΩ
ΕΨΗΛΑΦΗСΑΝ ΠΕΡΙ ΤΟΥ ΛΟΓΟΥ
ΤΗС ΖΩΗС· ΚΑΙ Η ΖΩΗ ΕΦΑΝΕΡΩ
ΘΗ ΚΑΙ ΕΩΡΑΚΑΜΕΝ ΚΑΙ ΜΑΡΤΥ
ΡΟΥΜΕΝ ΚΑΙ ΑΠΑΓΓΕΛΛΟΜΕΝ
ΥΜΙΝ ΤΗΝ ΖΩΗΝ ΤΗΝ ΑΙΩΝΙΟ
ΗΤΙС ΗΝ ΠΡΟС ΤΟΝ Π̅Ρ̅Α̅ ΚΑΙ ΕΦΑ
ΝΕΡΩΘΗ ΗΜΙΝ Ο ΕΩΡΑΚΑΜΕ
ΚΑΙ ΑΚΗΚΟΑΜΕΝ ΑΠΑΓΓΕΛΛΟ
ΜΕΝ ΚΑΙ ΥΜΙΝ ΙΝΑ ΚΑΙ ΥΜΕΙС
ΚΟΙΝΩΝΙΑΝ ΕΧΗΤΕ ΜΕΘ ΗΜΩ
ΚΑΙ Η ΚΟΙΝΩΝΙΑ ΔΕ Η ΗΜΕΤΕΡΑ
ΜΕΤΑ ΤΟΥ Π̅Ρ̅С̅ ΚΑΙ ΜΕΤΑ ΤΟΥ Υ̅Υ̅
ΑΥΤΟΥ Ι̅Υ̅ Χ̅Υ̅ ΚΑΙ ΤΑΥΤΑ ΓΡΑΦΟΜΕ
ΥΜΙΝ ΙΝΑ Η ΧΑΡΑ ΥΜΩΝ Η ΠΕ
ΠΛΗΡΩΜΕΝΗ
ΚΑΙ ΑΥΤΗ ΕСΤΙΝ Η ΑΓΓΕΛΙΑ
ΗΝ ΑΚΗΚΟΑΜΕΝ ΑΠ ΑΥΤΟΥ ΚΑΙ ΑΝ
ΓΕΛΛΟΜΕΝ ΥΜΙΝ ΟΤΙ Ο Θ̅С̅ ΦΩС
ΕСΤΙΝ ΚΑΙ СΚΟΤΙΑ ΕΝ ΑΥΤΩ ΟΥΚ
ΟΥΔΕΜΙΑ ΕΑΝ ΤΑΡΩΜΕΝ
ΟΤΙ ΚΟΙΝΩΝΙΑΝ ΕΧΟΜΕΝ ΜΕΤ ΑΥ
ΤΟΥ ΚΑΙ ΕΝ ΤΩ СΚΟΤΕΙ ΠΕΡΙΠΑ
ΤΩΜΕΝ ΨΕΥΔΟΜΕΘΑ ΚΑΙ ΟΥ ΠΟΙ
ΩΜΕΝ ΤΗΝ ΑΛΗΘΕΙΑΝ ΕΑΝ ΔΕ
ΕΝ ΤΩ ΦΩΤΙ ΠΕΡΙΠΑΤΩΜΕ
ΩС ΑΥΤΟС ΕСΤΙΝ ΕΝ ΤΩ ΦΩΤΙ

ΚΟΙΝΩΝΙΑΝ ΕΧ
ΚΑΙ ΤΟ ΑΙΜΑ Ι̅Υ̅
ΤΟΥ Κ̅Υ̅ ΚΑΘΑΡΙΖΕ
СΗС ΑΜΑΡΤΙΑС
Ο ΤΙ ΑΜΑΡΤΙΑΝ ΟΥ
ΕΑΥΤΟΥС ΠΛΑΝ
ΑΛΗΘΕΙΑ ΕΝ ΗΜ
ΕΑΝ ΟΜΟΛΟΓΩ
ΤΙΑС ΗΜΩΝ ΠΙ
ΚΑΙ ΔΙΚΑΙΟС ΙΝ
ΤΑС ΑΜΑΡΤΙΑС
ΗΜΑС ΑΠΟ ΠΑС
ΕΑΝ ΕΙΠΩΜΕ
ΤΗ ΚΑΜΕΝ· ΕΥ
ΜΕΝ ΑΥΤΟΝ ΚΑ
ΟΥΚ ΕСΤΙΝ ΕΝ
ΕΚΝΙΑ ΜΟΥ ΤΑΥ
ΙΝΑ ΜΗ ΑΜΑΡΤΗ
ΑΜΑΡΤΗ ΠΑΡΑΚ
ΠΡΟС ΤΟΝ Π̅Ρ̅Α̅
ΚΑΙ ΑΥΤΟС ΙΛΑС
Τ ΕΡΙ ΤΩΝ ΑΜΑ
ΟΥΤ ΕΡΙ ΤΩΝ ΗΜΕ
ΜΟΝΟΝ ΑΛΛΑ Κ
ΤΟΥ ΚΟСΜΟΥ Κ
ΓΙΝΩСΚΟΜΕ
ΜΕΝ ΑΥΤΟΝ ΕΑ
ΑΥΤΟΥ ΤΗΡΩΜ
Ο ΛΕΓΩΝ ΟΤΙ ΕΓΝ
ΚΑΙ ΤΑС ΕΝΤΟΛ
ΤΗΡΩΝ ΨΕΥСΤ
ΕΝ ΤΟΥΤΩ Η ΑΛΗ
ΘΕΑ ΟΥΚ ΕСΤΙΝ
ΤΟΥΟΥ ΤΕΤΕΛΕ
ΤΩ ΓΙΝΩСΚΟ
ΤΩ ΕСΜΕΝ
ΟС ΑΝ ΕΙΝΟ Φ
ΕΚΕΙΝΟС ΠΕΡΙ
ΚΑΙ ΑΥΤΟС ΕС
ΑΓΑΠΗΤΟΙ ΟΥΚ
ΓΡΑΦΩ ΥΜΙΝ
ΠΑΛΑΙΑΝ ΗΝ Ε
ΠΕΝ ΕΝΤΟΛΗ ΠΑ
ΛΟΝ ΟΝ ΗΚΟΥС
ΠΑΛΙΝ ΕΝΤΟΛΗΝ
ΥΜΙΝ Ο ΕСΤΙΝ
Θ̅С̅ ΚΑΙ ΕΝ ΗΜ
ΠΑΡΑΓΕΤΑΙ ΚΑΙ
ΟΘ Φ . . . . ΦΩС
ΕΝ ΤΩ ΦΩΤΙ Ε

TWO

How the Bible Was Written

•

THIS IS AN IMPOSSIBLY OPTIMISTIC TITLE for a short chapter in a very short introduction. Nevertheless, we need to say something about the processes by which the books we have in our Bibles came to be set down. How did they come to have their present form? This chapter will be very selective and take just a few examples, to stand for the very rich material that the Bible contains.

First, a few general remarks need to be made, starting with the time span during which the texts were being written. The earliest portions of the Old Testament are held to date from the tenth or eleventh century BCE (the poem in Judges 5), while the latest (the book of Daniel), comes

This page from the Codex Alexandrinus, a biblical manuscript in Greek created some time at the end of the fourth or the beginning of the fifth century CE, contains the end of 2 Peter and the beginning of 1 John. The Codex Alexandrinus is one of the earliest and most complete manuscripts of the Old and New Testaments in existence. Whereas it is bound in four volumes, earlier codices would have been much smaller and simpler, though they may have contained all four Gospels.

from the Maccabean period of the second century BCE. The time span for the New Testament is much shorter. The earliest of Paul's letters stems from ca. 50 CE; the majority of the rest of the texts certainly fall within the first century. The latest date seriously put forward for any of the NT books would be around the mid-second century for 2 Peter, though it may well date from the first quarter. This helps to make the obvious point that the biblical texts were produced over a period in which the living conditions of the writers—political, cultural, economic, and ecological— varied enormously. There are texts which reflect a nomadic existence, texts from people with an established monarchy and Temple cult, texts from exile, texts born out of fierce oppression by foreign rulers, courtly texts, texts from wandering charismatic preachers, texts from those who give themselves the airs of sophisticated Hellenistic writers. It is a time span which encompasses the compositions of Homer, Plato, Aristotle, Thucydides, Sophocles, Caesar, Cicero, and Catullus. It is a period which sees the rise and fall of the Assyrian empire (twelfth to seventh century) and of the Persian empire (sixth to fourth century), Alexander's campaigns (336–326), the rise of Rome and its domination of the Mediterranean (fourth century to the founding of the Principate, 27 BCE), the destruction of the Jerusalem Temple (70 CE), and the extension of Roman rule to parts of Scotland (84 CE).

Orality and Literacy

One thing that these texts, so widely separated in time, do have in common is their location in a culture in which writing was highly valued, even if its practice was still largely in the hands of specialists. The period of the composition of the earliest biblical texts broadly corresponds with the advance from cuneiform writing to the use of an

This cuneiform inscription on a hill near the ancient Fortress of Van, just west of modern-day Van, Turkey, contains a paean to the Babylonian god Ahuramazda from the Persian king Xerxes the Great (reigned 485–65 BCE). Cuneiform tablets and cylinders were the predecessors to the modern alphabet, which, together with the development of materials like papyrus, made possible the creation of the world's first major literary texts, such as those collected in the Bible.

alphabet. In cuneiform writing, words are represented by signs incised into clay tablets by a wedge-shaped instrument. In the earliest alphabets, which originate with the Phoenicians, consonants are inscribed in ink on papyrus or some such suitable material. This was both more flexible and more portable. Above all, it made it possible to produce much longer texts. Texts in the new alphabet could be written on scrolls, which were usually made of leather and could encompass all the sixty-six chapters of Isaiah. The later development of the codex (roughly corresponding to our present book format) made for greater ease of reference and portability. A codex would permit the inclusion of all four Gospels within the same covers, producing a volume about two and a half times the length of this book. Its use as a medium for literary texts, pioneered by the early Christians, dates from the first century CE. It became standard from about the fourth century.

The development of new techniques of recording language was one of the most remarkable technological features of this time, comparable in importance to the development of the printing press in the sixteenth century, which made possible the rapid spread of Reformation ideas. However, for the most part culture during the biblical period remained

· · · · ·

TABLE ILLUSTRATING THE DEVELOPMENT OF CUNEIFORM SIGN FORMS OVER MORE THAN TWO THOUSAND YEARS

					SAG Head
					NINDA Bread
					GU₇ Eat
					AB₂ Cow
					APIN Plough
					SUHUR Carp
Ca. 3100 BCE (Uruk IV)	**Ca. 3000 BCE (Uruk III)**	**Ca. 2500 BCE (Fara)**	**Ca. 2100 BCE (Ur III)**	**Ca. 700 BCE (Neo-Assyrian)**	**Sumerian reading + meaning**

· · · · ·

oral. That is to say, written texts were mostly communicated by being read aloud: the majority of those who received the texts would have heard rather than read them. Moreover, most of the material we now have in written form, whether legal, prophetic, proverbial, poetic, or narrative, will have started out in oral form and only subsequently been committed to writing. So, for example, prophetic oracles were delivered orally by the prophet, committed to memory by the prophet's disciples, and then later written down. Between the initial oracles, their subsequent writing down, their collection together with other similar material, and their eventual publication in the form of a prophetic book, a period of several centuries may have elapsed, as in the case of the book of Isaiah. Even where texts were produced by one person, as in the case of the Pauline epistles, they were often dictated to a scribe, though Paul on occasion added his own greetings himself: "See with what large letters I am writing to you with my own hand" (Galatians 6:11).

Thus throughout the period of the composition of the Bible orality and literacy are closely interrelated. This is reflected in the fact that there are different degrees of literateness among the texts: some come from circles where there is a high degree of proficiency in the composing of written texts, while others are much closer to the oral recitation of narratives and discourses. This can be easily illustrated from the Gospels: Mark's Gospel is generally agreed to be the earliest of the four and is also the least literate, both in the roughness of its Greek style and in the closeness of its contents to the oral tradition of stories and sayings about Jesus. Luke, by contrast, tells us quite clearly that he is writing as a Greek historian who has sifted his sources carefully and is writing a reliable, literary account (Luke 1:1–4). His style is noticeably literary, echoing the particular character of the Greek translation of the Hebrew scriptures.

LUKE AND MARK

Luke starts his Gospel by explaining why and how he has written it. There have been other attempts at recording what happened in the life of Jesus. He, like a good historian, has sifted through them and has produced a reliable account.

Luke's Preface to His Gospel

Inasmuch as many have undertaken to compile a narrative of the things which have been accomplished among us, just as they were delivered to us by those who from the beginning were eyewitnesses and ministers of the word, it seemed good to me also, having followed all things closely for some time past, to write an orderly account for you, most excellent Theophilus, that you may know the truth concerning the things of which you have been informed (Luke 1:1–4).

Mark, by contrast, starts with a simple assertion: "The beginning of the gospel of Jesus Christ, the Son of God." It is a little difficult to illustrate contrasting styles in translation but some idea can be gained from the following:

Mark 1:1–8

The beginning of the gospel of Jesus Christ, the Son of God. As it is written in Isaiah the prophet, "Behold, I send my messenger before thy face, who shall prepare thy way; the voice of one crying in the wilderness: Prepare the way of the Lord, make his paths straight—" John the baptizer appeared in the wilderness, preaching a baptism of repentance for the forgiveness of sins.

Luke 3:1–6

In the fifteenth year of the reign of Tiberius Caesar, Pontius Pilate being governor of Judea, and Herod being tetrarch of Galilee, and his brother Philip tetrarch of the region of Ituraea and Trachonitis, and Lysanias tetrarch of Abilene, in the high-priesthood of Annas and Caiaphas, the word of God came to John the son of Zechariah in the wilderness; and he went into all the region about the Jordan, preaching a baptism of repentance for the forgiveness of sins. As it is written in the book of the words of Isaiah the prophet, "The voice of one crying in the wilderness: Prepare the way of the Lord, make his paths straight."

Luke tends to write in long, literary sentences with subordinate phrases and clauses (hypotactic style). He sets the account of Jesus's baptism in its historical, political context. Mark's Greek is characterized by sentences consisting of a number of main clauses simply linked with "and" (paratactic style), which is a characteristic of oral story-telling. Whereas Luke first locates John in Roman history, Mark relates his coming only to scriptural prophecy, and has some difficulty handling the syntax when including the citation from the prophets. The quotation simply runs on into the clause about John's appearance in the wilderness.

· · · · ·

The Bible's Literary World

What was the actual process of composition of the biblical texts within this overall context of literacy and orality? One needs to bear in mind that the biblical writers would have approached their task in a very different way from, say,

Each of the four Gospels in the New Testament describes the role of John the Baptist in announcing the arrival of Jesus Christ—in fulfillment, as they insist, of Old Testament scriptures. This painting by Pieter Brueghel the Younger from 1601 depicts John preaching in a woodland overlooking a river—more like the Rhine than the Jordan—to a group of people from all walks of life.

a modern novelist. The novelist is to a large measure in control of her material, creating a literary whole from her imagination and experience, drawing on literary allusions and traditions as she will. By contrast, the ancient writers of religious texts are much more constrained by the deposits of the past, whether oral or literary. They are as much compilers as they are makers of texts.

It is not necessary to read more than a couple of chapters of the book of Genesis to begin to sense what a different literary world one has entered. In the first chapter we learn how God created the world over six days and rested on the seventh. The narrative starts with a description of chaos and darkness and builds up, through the creation of the heavenly bodies, land and seas, plants and animals, to its climax in the creation of man and woman.

"God created man in his own image, in the image of God he created him; male and female he created them." (Genesis 1:27). The story stresses the goodness of creation, its worth in and of itself, before man and woman even come on the scene. This is not to deny the strong sense of human domination over the created world which is expressed in v. 28. But even so there is a limit to human domination. In Genesis 1 both human beings and animals are strictly vegetarian. (It is only after the flood, in Genesis 9:3–4, that human beings are permitted to become carnivores.) The story finishes with God resting from his labors, contemplating everything that he has made, "and behold, it was very good."

So far there is nothing very remarkable to alert us to the different literary world which we have entered. But in 2:4 the story starts again, and in a rather different form. In the first place, the story is differently structured: the device of days which was used in chapter one is absent. Then, too, the order of events is very different: after a brief account of the creation of the heavens and the earth (very different from the emphasis on their creation in chapter one, where four days elapse before the creation of any animate beings), we are given a picture of an earth void of all vegetation, "for the LORD God had not caused it to rain upon the earth, and there was no man to till the ground" (2:5). God causes a mist to come up and water the earth and then as his first action creates man/ Adam (the Hebrew "Adam" is both the word for "human being" and a name). But, while the term is generic, Adam is a male and very much on his own. The rest of the story is then structured around God's provision of succor and support for him. First, God creates a garden for the man, with plants and trees for food, with the exception of the tree of knowledge of good and evil. Then he creates the animals to be Adam's companions. But even these are not enough. So finally God puts Adam to sleep and creates from his rib a woman, and Adam is content, for the time being at least. The story finishes with the man and woman together, blissfully ignorant of their nakedness.

The differences in these two accounts are striking. The second account represents God in frankly human terms, places human beings at the center of creation, and, in its story of woman's creation out of Adam's rib, vividly symbolizes women's subordination to men. Like a sculptor, God models man out of dust; like some kind of Frankenstein, he puts man to sleep and takes out a rib and turns it into a woman. How different from the loftier account of God's agency in chapter one: "And God said, 'Let there be light'; and there was light" (1:3), a motif which is repeated throughout the chapter. Again, chapter two makes the whole purpose of creation rotate around man's (*sic*!) needs. Everything is put there for man's purpose and without man nothing will be brought into existence.

The story of God's creation of Adam and Eve occurs twice in the first two chapters of the Old Testament book of Genesis. The latter account focuses on the human place in God's creation, and on Adam and Eve's life in the Garden of Eden. The creation of Eve out of Adam's side is vividly depicted in this woodcut from the Nuremberg Chronicles, an illustrated world history first published in 1493.

In chapter one human beings are indeed the crowning glory of creation, but are still very much a part of the whole process. Finally, chapter two's account of human creation is unashamedly male-oriented: man's creation is put first and everything subsequent depends on him. Woman's creation comes right at the end, a last resort, which rapidly goes badly wrong.

One final difference, which is not readily apparent from the English translation. In the first chapter God is referred to by the Hebrew *elohim*, which is actually a plural form. In the second, he is additionally referred to as YHWH (probably to be read as Yahweh, but the original vowels were not written).

That is to say, we have here two versions of the same story, which use different terminology for no less important a character than God, and which contain a considerable measure of inconsistency over the order of creation, over men and women's relation to it, and indeed over the question of man and woman's relation to each other.

Such phenomena are repeated over and over again throughout the first five books of the Bible. For instance, there are different, and somewhat contradictory, accounts of, the flood (cf. Genesis 7:2, 3 with 6:19; 7:8, 9, 15), Abraham's migration (Genesis 12:1–4a; 12:4b–5), God's covenant with Abraham (Genesis 15 and 17), the manna and quail in the wilderness (Exodus 16:2–3, 6–35a; Numbers 11:4–34), the Ten Commandments (Exodus 20:1–17; 34:10–28; Deuteronomy 5:6–18), and the dietary rules prohibiting the eating of certain animals (Leviticus 11 and Deuteronomy 14). In addition to differences in narrative, there are further examples of differences in terminology. In some accounts Sinai is the mountain of the covenant (e.g. Exodus 19:1; 24:16); in others it is Horeb (Deuteronomy 4:10; 5:2). Some stories favor certain Hebrew words, for example relating to dying, the plague, the congregation, which occur rarely, if at all, in the parallel stories. That is to say, parallel versions of stories exist and these parallels can be sorted into groups with a largely consistent use of certain terms.

· · · · ·

DOUBLETS IN THE HEBREW BIBLE

A number of stories occur in two versions in the Bible. Different oral traditions have been recorded and then included in the final version of the text. Sometimes, as in the story of Abraham's journey to Canaan, they are simply put in one after the other; on other occasions, as with the story of the animals in the ark, they have been interwoven with each other and have to be reconstructed by the scholar.

Abraham's Migration

Genesis 12:1–4a

Now the LORD said to Abram, "Go from your country and your kindred and your father's house to the land that I will show you. And I will make of you a great nation, and I will bless you, and make your name great, so that you will be a blessing. I will bless those who bless you, and him who curses you I will curse; and by you all the families of the earth shall bless themselves." So Abram went, as the LORD had told him; and Lot went with him. Abram was seventy-five years old when he departed from Haran.

Genesis 12:4b–5

And Abram took Sarai his wife, and Lot his brother's son, and all their possessions which they had gathered, and the persons that they had gotten in Haran; and they set forth to go to the land of Canaan.

Instructions to Noah About the Animals

Genesis 7:2–3

Take with you seven pairs of all clean animals, the male and his mate; and a pair of the animals that are not clean, the male and his mate; and seven pairs of the birds of the air also, male and female, to keep their kind alive upon the face of all the earth.

Genesis 6:19; 7:8–9

And of every living thing of all flesh, you shall bring two of every sort into the ark, to keep them alive with you; they shall be male and female. Of clean animals, and of animals that are not clean, and of birds, and of everything that creeps on the ground, two and two, male and female, went into the ark with Noah, as God had commanded Noah. They went into the ark with Noah, two and two of all flesh in which there was the breath of life.

· · · · ·

The much-loved story of Noah's Ark contains conflicting details about the number of pairs of animals to be taken into the Ark: was it a pair of each? Or was it seven pairs of clean animals and only one pair of the unclean? This painting of the Ark and its animal passengers comes from the Abbey Church of Saint-Savin-sur-Gartempe in Saint-Savin, France. Its murals date from the mid-eleventh century and, as is traditional, depict no more than one of each kind of animal.

SOURCES FOR THE FIVE BOOKS OF THE PENTATEUCH: GENESIS, EXODUS, LEVITICUS, NUMBERS, DEUTERONOMY

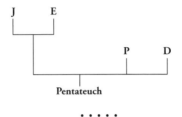

. . . . .

What are we to make of all this? The consensus of scholarship is that the stories are taken from four different written sources and that these were brought together over the course of time to form the first five books of the Bible as a composite work. The sources are known as J, the Jahwist source (from the German transliteration of the Hebrew YHWH), E, the Elohist source, P, the priestly source, and D, the Deuteronomist source. It is thought that first J and E were combined and then at a later stage P was fitted into the narrative framework of the combined J+E; then D was added as the fifth book, perhaps at the same time as P was incorporated, with some adjustments to the placing of the story of Joshua's commissioning. The earliest material goes back to the eleventh century. The final compilation dates from the fifth century, and may include revisions reflecting overall the views of P. Thus the Pentateuch (or Torah, as it is known by Jews) comprises material taken from six centuries of human history, which has been put together to give a comprehensive picture of the creation of the world and of God's dealings with his peoples, specifically with the people of Israel.

· · · · ·

YHWH

This is a term which occurs a significant number of times, but not by any means uniformly, through out the Hebrew Bible. In the texts which are vocalized, the vowels added are taken from the Hebrew word for Lord, *adonai*. Read with these vowels, the consonants YHWH give something like JeHoVaH. The original vocalization was probably Yahweh (sometimes Jahweh), but the actual form has not been preserved. Jews had a profound sense of respect and awe for the divine name and therefore avoided its use, preferring alternatives such as "Lord." The occurrence of different forms of the divine name is used by scholars as a means of identifying the major literary sources which contributed to the Pentateuch.

· · · · ·

It is not only the books of the Old Testament which have their origins in a variety of oral and literary traditions. The same is true of the Gospels. The Gospels represent four tellings of Jesus's life, death, and resurrection, with interesting differences of perspective and detail, though also with considerable agreement. In the case of the first three, Matthew, Mark, and Luke, the agreements are remarkable. It is not just that they agree about the order of many events and in much of the detail of what occurred. It is even more that they agree, in the case of individual sections, in the overall literary structure of the narrative, and in sentence structure, choice of words, and grammatical forms. These linguistic agreements are so striking that they almost force one to the conclusion that there is literary dependence of one kind or another. That is to say, someone has been copying someone else.

The usual, though by no means undisputed, view is that Mark wrote first, and that Matthew and Luke both used Mark and another source consisting mainly of sayings attributed to Jesus and referred to as Q. This then allows the historian of early Christianity to reconstruct different theological perspectives associated with the different Gospels and also with Q.

Each of the four Evangelists—Matthew, Mark, Luke, and John, the traditional authors of the four Gospels—is associated with a symbol, which often accompanies the portraits of the Evangelists in Christian art. Some scholars believe that the symbols derive from Revelation 4:6–8, which describes four living creatures standing next to the throne of God. This thirteenth-century carving on the lid of an ivory box depicts Christ in majesty surrounded by an angel (Matthew), a winged lion (Mark), a winged ox (Luke), and an eagle (John).

· · · · ·

THE TAX COLLECTOR

These accounts of the calling of a tax collector show a remarkable verbal agreement, which is most easily explained if two of the three accounts have been copied from the third. It is also interesting to note the differences, which may indicate changes of understanding and emphasis on the part of the different writers.

Matthew 9:9–13

As Jesus passed on from there, he saw a man called Matthew sitting at the tax office; and he said to him, "Follow me." And he rose and followed him. And as he sat at table in the house, behold, many tax collectors and sinners came and sat down with Jesus and his disciples. And when the Pharisees saw this, they said to his disciples, "Why does your teacher eat with tax collectors and sinners?" But when he heard it, he said, "Those who are well have no need of a physician, but those who are sick. Go and learn what this means, 'I desire mercy, and not sacrifice.' For I came not to call the righteous, but sinners."

Mark 2:13–17

He went out again beside the sea; and all the crowd gathered about him, and he taught them. And as he passed on, he saw Levi the son of Alphaeus sitting at the tax office, and he said to him, "Follow me." And he rose and followed him. And as he sat at table in his house, many tax collectors and sinners were sitting with Jesus and his disciples; for there were many who followed him. And the scribes of the Pharisees, when they saw that he was eating with sinners and tax collectors, said to his disciples, "Why does he eat with tax collectors and sinners?" And when Jesus heard it, he said to them, "Those who are well have no need of a physician, but those who are sick; I came not to call the righteous, but sinners."

Luke 5:27–32

After this he went out, and saw a tax collector, named Levi, sitting at the tax office; and he said to him, "Follow me." And he left everything, and rose and followed him. And Levi made him a great feast in his house; and there was a large company of tax collectors and others sitting at table with them. And the Pharisees and their scribes murmured against his disciples, saying, "Why do you eat and drink with tax collectors and sinners?" And Jesus answered them, "Those who are well have no need of a physician, but those who are sick; I have not come to call the righteous, but sinners to repentance."

· · · · ·

But that is not quite the end of the story. What about the earliest Gospel, Mark? Where did he get his material from? Behind Mark must lie oral traditions which he collected and put into some kind of order. Similarly, the material ascribed to Q (broadly the sayings which Matthew and Luke have in common) may also have been in oral, not written, form.

Scholars have attempted to reconstruct something of the history of the oral traditions behind the Gospels, but the results have not been too encouraging. The period of transmission is short: less than forty years passed between the death of Jesus and the writing of Mark's Gospel. This means that there was little time for oral traditions to assume fixed form, though it is likely that there was an extended oral narrative of the last days of Jesus, which was probably used in Christian worship and formed the basis of the various accounts of Jesus's death (the Passion narratives) in the Gospels. Even so, it is difficult to know which elements of

The four major accounts of the life and death of Jesus Christ contain many parallels. To keep track of where each Gospel agrees with or differs from the others, Eusebius, bishop of Caesarea (ca. 265–340; see pages 67–68), devised what is now called a canon table, which lists the various stories in the Gospels according to their occurrence in the four books. Those that occur in all four Gospels are listed first; those in Matthew, Mark, and Luke next, and so on. This canon table comes from the Rabbula Gospels, an illuminated manuscript of the four Gospels created around 586 CE at the Monastery of St. John of Zagba in western Asia. Kings Solomon and David appear at the upper left and right; scenes from the life of Christ appear below.

Mark's Gospel (or indeed of the hypothetical Q) come from the tradition and which from Mark himself.

What one can say with some confidence though is that it is likely that stories and sayings about Jesus circulated in varying oral forms before they were written down. The Gospels, like the Hebrew Bible, have their roots in an oral culture. Nevertheless, while they resemble the Hebrew Bible in that respect, there is also an impressive rush to literacy in the Gospels. Four major literary accounts of the life, death, and resurrection of Jesus within a period of around forty years is a remarkable achievement. It is a clear indication of the growing importance of literary production in all levels of society in the first-century Mediterranean world. It is also indicative of the early Christians' desire to be part of that society, despite their beliefs in an imminent and dramatic end to the world as they knew it.

That is to say, many of the books of the Bible are not the work of one author, written over a period of a few years; rather they are compilations which reflect communal traditions which may go back many centuries. Even in the case of the New Testament, where admittedly there is a much greater preponderance of works written by a single author, the Gospels are still in an important sense communal productions, which preserve the traditions of the earliest Christians.

Yet, even though the writings of the Bible have deep roots in an oral culture and tradition, they are also clearly literary works. In the first place, they use literary forms and conventions. The Bible contains a great variety of such forms. The Hebrew Bible is traditionally divided into three parts: the Torah, the Prophets, and the Writings. The Torah (or Pentateuch) comprises the first five books and contains a mixture of narratives and legal texts. In some sections narrative predominates (Genesis, Exodus,

APPROXIMATE DATES OF NEW TESTAMENT BOOKS
AND CONTEMPORARY WRITERS

	New Testament Books	Contemporary Greek and Latin Writers
49	1 Thessalonians	Philo of Alexandria, Jewish
		Hellenistic philosopher
52–54	Galatians	(15 BCE–50 CE)
	1 Corinthians	Plutarch, Greek historian,
		philosopher, and writer
		(46–120)
55–56	2 Corinthians	Epictetus, Greek Stoic
		philosopher
	Romans	(50–138)
60–62	Philemon	Juvenal, Roman satirical writer
		(58–138)
	Philippians	Seneca, Roman Stoic
		philosopher, commits suicide
		on Nero's order (65)
68–70	Mark	Petronius, Roman satirical
		novelist, commits suicide (66)
75–90	Matthew, Luke, Acts	Martial, Roman epigrammatic
		poet (40–104)
90s	John, 1, 2, 3 John, Jude	
95–96	Revelation (41–100)	
100–130	2 Peter	

Other books can be dated broadly in the last three decades of the first century CE:

Colossians

Ephesians

Hebrews

1 and 2 Timothy, Titus

James

· · · · ·

and Numbers); in others the legal material is dominant (Leviticus and Deuteronomy). Deuteronomy is cast as the last testament of Moses to the people, prior to his death and the entry of the people into the Land under Joshua. The Prophets contains prophetic books with both narrative and prophetic oracles, preceded by the histories of Joshua, Judges, Samuel, and Kings. These books contain masterpieces of storytelling, but also construct a history of the people with a distinctive theological

The Torah, or the first five books of the Bible, is the most holy of Jewish scriptures. This *sefer* Torah—a Torah written by hand on a parchment scroll by a specially trained and qualified scribe—comes from the former Glockengasse synagogue in Cologne, Germany, now the Cologne Opera House. The synagogue was destroyed by the Nazis on Kristallnacht in 1938.

perspective. The Writings contains a mixture of psalms, proverbial material, and more historical books.

The New Testament adds a number of forms to this: Gospels, which bear considerable resemblance to contemporary biographies or "Lives"; letters, which vary from the fairly short personal communication (Philemon) to the elaborate treatise of sixteen chapters in Paul's Letter to the Romans; acts, a form recording the deeds of famous figures which would have many exemplars in Christian literature; and an apocalypse, Revelation, a contemporary form which enjoyed considerable popularity in first-century Judaism. The writers and compilers of the Bible, that is to say, used a variety of literary forms in which to cast their works. Many of these forms may have had their origins in popular, oral culture, but within the tradition of biblical writing and compilation such literary forms became influential and constrained the way in which the books were written. Even the Gospel form, which may, as a particular variation of the contemporary Life, be ascribed to Mark, was immediately emulated by the other canonical evangelists and by many others whose works were never included in the canon. The Bible both drew on and created literary traditions and forms.

Literary Allusions within the Bible

This consciousness of working within a literary tradition is reflected in the way the writers refer back to earlier books in the Bible. It is natural that in recording the lives and deeds of the great figures of their people's history writers should make comparisons. Even though, as Deuteronomy says, "there has not arisen a prophet since in Israel like Moses, whom the Lord knew face to face, none like him for all the signs and the wonders which the Lord sent him to do . . ." (Deuteronomy 34:10–11), that does not deter later writers from at least attempting to make comparisons. Thus, when Joshua, whom Moses had commissioned to lead the people into the Promised Land, comes with the Ark of the Covenant to the Jordan, the allusions to the Crossing of the Red Sea are clear. In both cases the people camp before the waters and then move out in the morning. In both cases there is a miraculous parting of the waters, so that the waters form a wall (Exodus 14:21–22), "stand in one heap" (Joshua 3:13, 16). In all this, however, Joshua does as Moses has told him, and the people "stand in awe of him, as they had stood in awe of Moses, all the days of his life" (4:14). Similar points of comparison can be made between the story of Gideon's call in Judges 6 and Moses's call in Exodus 3. Judges refers back explicitly to the Exodus, 6:7–10, 13. There are similarities in language: "I will be with you" (Judges 6:16, cf. Exodus 3:12). Furthermore, there are structural similarities between the two stories: the oppression of Israel, the call of the deliverer, the ruin of foreign deities, a holy war. These points of comparison are developed further in later retellings.

Allusions in biblical books to events described in previous books is common. The story of Joshua at the Jordan in Joshua 3, for example, echoes the story of Moses and the Israelites crossing the Red Sea in Exodus 14. The Armenian artist Toros Roslin (ca. 1210–70) painted this depiction of Moses parting the waters for a medieval Armenian Bible.

The process does not however stop with the Old Testament writings. It is continued in the retelling of these stories in extra-biblical Hebrew and Greek literature and in the New Testament. The infancy stories in Matthew contain quotations and more indirect allusions to the Moses birth story.

What these brief examples show is a living religious tradition where the textual tradition is in dialogue with itself. What is fixed as revelation in one book is taken up and interpreted in later writings. The range of this kind of literary interplay is certainly much wider than can be illustrated here. The figure of Moses runs through the narratives of the Bible,

· · · · ·

LITERARY ALLUSIONS

Biblical writers often draw on earlier narratives and literary motifs in shaping their own accounts. Here we see the close connections between Exodus 4:19–21 and Matthew 2:19–20.

Exodus 4:19–21

And the LORD said to Moses in Midian, "Go back to Egypt; for all the men who were seeking your life are dead." So Moses took his wife and his sons and set them on an ass, and went back to the land of Egypt; and in his hand Moses took the rod of God.

Matthew 2:19–20

But when Herod died, behold, an angel of the Lord appeared in a dream to Joseph in Egypt, saying, "Rise, take the child and his mother, and go to the land of Israel, for those who sought the child's life are dead." And he rose and took the child and his mother, and went to the land of Israel.

· · · · ·

shaping the way the stories are told, used as a standard by which to judge subsequent characters in the narrative. Similarly the story of the Exodus, the desert wanderings, and the capture of the Land will return again to shape legal, prophetic, and liturgical material. The great events of the past as told in sacred scripture inevitably affect the way the present is experienced and the future dreamed of. The theme of the entry into the Land after the desert wanderings will emerge in the prophecies of Isaiah to encourage those in exile to hope for return, to look for the glorious restoration of Israel, when all nations will flock to pay homage to Zion, to the restored glory of Temple and nation (see Isaiah 40:1–11, 60:1–14).

The same visions shaped the beliefs of Jews at the time of Christ's birth. The Qumran sectarians, the authors of the Dead Sea Scrolls, saw going out into the desert as a preparation for the final restoration of Israel and the renewal of the Temple. In Mark John the Baptist opens the Gospel by proclaiming "the way of the Lord." He is of course pointing to his own baptism, which is to prepare the way for Jesus, the stronger one who will come after him to baptize with the Holy Spirit and with fire.

It is interesting to reflect on the very different contexts in which these texts were shaped. The text from Isaiah comes from the period of Israel's exile in Babylonia. It promises to those whose lives have been uprooted a return to the Land and to their former glories. Indeed their glory will be greater: all nations will come to acknowledge the glory of the Lord. By contrast, the Qumran sectarians lived in inner exile in the Land, seeing both the Roman occupying forces and the Temple priests as being ruled over by the spirit of darkness. Their world has again been overturned by foreign forces who have robbed them of their independence and under-mined their religious traditions; but they have also lost confidence in the religious leaders of the nation. They too embrace the prophetic hope for a return to the founding moments of Jewish history; however, they look not for a physical return from exile, but for the overthrow of the occupying forces and a restoration and renewal of the Temple and its priesthood.

In the Gospel of Mark, the sense of these ancient prophecies is extended still further. Mark, writing for a persecuted community of Gentile Christians in Rome, is in no way concerned with the renewal or restoration of Israel and the Jerusalem Temple. For him the "way of the Lord" leads from the desert via Jesus's ministry of preaching, healing, and exorcising to Jerusalem, where Jesus is crucified and the veil of the Temple is torn. The disciples are then told to return to Galilee, from where they will go out to preach the gospel to all nations. The problems faced by Mark's Gentile community, barbaric public torture and execution, are no longer peculiar

This photograph taken in the hills in the Judaean desert overlooking the Dead Sea shows one of the caves in which the scrolls from the community at Qumran were found.

．．．．．

The Qumran sectarians were a group whose writings, the Dead Sea Scrolls, were first sensationally discovered in caves near Wadi Qumran in 1947. They were (probably) a group which had split from the resistance party formed in opposition to the Seleucid overlords in the early second century BCE. They lived a strictly regulated, celibate life on the shores of the Dead Sea at Kirbhet Qumran, where they produced a large library of biblical manuscripts and commentaries, along with their own legal, liturgical, and prophetic material. They expected a holy war after which the Romans would be defeated and Israel restored. The community was destroyed during the Jewish War in 68 CE.

．．．．．

to a particular nation. As such their resolution can no longer be conceived in terms of national restoration. For Mark, the resolution of these problems lies in Jesus's binding of Satan and his calling people to be with him (3:14) and to preach this good news to all nations (13:10).

A Living Oral and Literary Tradition

I have tried in this chapter to give some impression of the way in which the biblical books were composed. In particular I have been keen to stress their genesis in a period which saw the rise of literature but which was nevertheless still in many ways an oral culture. This marks the Bible as a collection of texts which has deep roots in the oral traditions of Jews and Christians. These texts were only gradually written down and this process itself would have been staged. The books we now have may have been based on or in fact incorporate other literary collections and documents.

The oral traditions, once written down, can influence the creation of further literary works, or the editing of new oral traditions which have been recorded. The earlier works of the Bible exert their influence on later writing and at the same time are reworked and even subverted by later writing. The tradition, oral or literary, is a dynamic and sometimes contentious one. It certainly does not speak with one voice, but the different voices speak the same language. They pick up phrases and motifs, they share a common stock of images and ideas which they republish in sometimes strikingly different ways. It is a lively and wide-ranging exchange, with stories and histories, debates about laws and regulations, proverbs and sayings, letters and visions. Such texts contain a rich vocabulary through which people in different situations and at different times may attempt to come to terms with their experiences of well-being or of suffering and oppression. These texts provide a rich source of legal, social, and political wisdom by which people may seek to order their affairs, to strengthen the nation, and to live with their neighbors. They are also the stuff of dreams. The great events of the past, of deliverance from bondage and of heroic perseverance in the desert, may be recreated in the future. New worlds may emerge which mirror the past and its glories in wholly surprising ways. This process of reappropriation and reworking of the texts which occurs within the biblical writings continues, as we shall see, in the subsequent history of their reception within Jewish and Christian communities.

THREE

The Making of the Bible

The Many Names of the Bible

So far I have been speaking fairly freely about "the Bible," without asking what might be meant by that expression. The word itself is derived from the Greek *biblia*, which is simply the plural form of *biblion*, book. The singularity of the expression "the Bible" conceals a sense of plurality in its etymological roots. The Bible is a collection of books: which books and why?

The Bishops' Bible, published in 1568, was the main precursor to the King James Version. It was in turn a revision of the earlier Great Bible, which was based largely on the Latin Vulgate (see page 54). Matthew Parker, Elizabeth's archbishop, assigned the work to a number of scholars, many of whom were or subsequently become bishops. They were encouraged to revise the Great Bible where it diverged from the Hebrew, though most only had access to this through Latin translations. In this title page from the 1569 quarto edition, Queen Elizabeth is surrounded by the allegorical figures of Justice, Mercy, Fortitude, and Prudence.

A dictionary defines it as: "Christian scriptures of the Old and New Testament; copy of them; particular edition of them (Bishops', Breeches, Printers', Vinegar, Wicked *Bible*); . . . authoritative book." This is doubtless the standard conventional sense of the name in English as it is spoken today in England (and in many other places) and it clearly reflects the influence of Christianity on that usage. It defines the Bible as consisting of two parts, the Old and the New Testaments; it indicates that the collection was intended as a source of authority; and it adds another twist: this collection comes in different versions or editions.

This, however, is not the only view of the nature of the collection. The expression, "the Bible," these days at least, also occurs in expressions such as "the Hebrew Bible," "the Jewish Bible," and the Christian Bible." It is quite clear that the Christian Bible contains much that is in the Jewish sacred scriptures, whether or not these are always referred to by Jews as "Bible."

Before we get into a discussion of the history of these different, though interconnected, collections of books, a word about nomenclature. We will start with the Jewish scriptures. The collection of writings which Jews regard as sacred has had many names. The most common are "scripture," "the scriptures," "the sacred scriptures," "the books," "the 24 books," "the Law, the Prophets, and the Writings," "Tanak" (an acronym based on the initial Hebrew letters of the words for the different sections of scripture—Torah, Nebiim, Ketubim), and "mikra" (literally, "what is read [aloud]"). The last two were established by the Middle Ages. Names such as "the Jewish Bible" and "the Hebrew Bible" are much more recent, though it is difficult to pin down their precise origin. They have quite recently become the subject of considerable attention in departments of religious studies, where titles like "the chair of Old Testament" seem inappropriate in a multicultural or multifaith context.

ROGUE EDITIONS OF THE BIBLE

Printers' errors and unusual translations have led to a number of versions of the Bible gaining nicknames. These are some of the better known:

Breeches Bible: The 1560 edition of the Geneva Bible with "breeches" for "aprons" in Genesis 3:7. This translation also occurred in Wycliff's Bible.

Printers' Bible: With "Printers" for "Princes" in Psalm 119:161, producing the, for the publishers, finely appropriate sentence: "Printers have persecuted me without a cause."

Vinegar Bible: 1717 edition with a running title for Luke 22 reading "the parable of the vinegar" for "vineyard."

Wicked Bible: 1632 edition where the seventh commandment reads: "Thou shalt commit adultery."

Christian usage has its roots in these Jewish names. In the New Testament writings we find references to "scripture" and "the scriptures," where the singular refers either to particular passages (sometimes "this scripture," e.g., Mark 12:10) or to scripture as a whole (e.g., Romans 4:3). This latter use is probably derived from the Greek translation of the Hebrew scriptures, known as the Septuagint. Here Hebrew expressions like "by the word of YHWH" are translated "by the word of God in scripture" (e.g.,

1 Chronicles 15:15). This usage is sustained in the subsequent tradition and as *sacra scriptura* is standard in the works of Thomas Aquinas, the great Catholic theologian of the Middle Ages, for example. It remains a favored way of referring to the Bible within Roman Catholic theological circles.

Sometimes in the New Testament, the Greek *biblion* (book) is used for the book of the Law (Galatians 3:10; Hebrews 9:19); here the writers again follow the usage of the Septuagint. However, other first-century Jewish writers in Greek, notably Josephus and Philo, predominantly use the plural *biblia* and it is this usage which becomes standard in later church usage, certainly from the later fourth century. It is only in the Middle Ages that the Latin borrowed word *biblia* comes to be treated as a singular expression and this is then reflected in subsequent linguistic usage in European languages: *la bible, la biblia, die Bibel*, etc.

So, to put it simply, the term "Bible," as a collection of sacred texts, is first used for the Christian scriptures, in their different versions. Only later is it used of Jewish scriptures in a manner which is designed to distinguish the Hebrew from the Christian scriptures. Thus the Bible, in most recent usage, is ambiguous: it may refer either to the Jewish or the Christian Bibles, in their various forms. Now we need to consider how these collections were made. What kind of diversity has the process of collecting and fixing the scriptures of the different Jewish and Christian communities produced?

The Making of the Jewish Canon: The Hebrew Bible and Its Greek Version

The process of collecting and fixing the scriptures of a particular community is often referred to as the canonization of scripture. The Greek word *kanon* means rod or reed, and, by extension, rule or measure.

To create a canon of sacred writings is to create a collection which will be in some sense normative for the community for which it is intended. A very important factor to bear in mind is that both Jewish and Christian scriptures were, from an early date, produced in different language versions. The process of collection and the process of translation were closely connected. For practical purposes, it will be convenient to look at the formation of the Hebrew Bible and its Greek version separately.

The Formation of the Hebrew Bible

As we have already seen, the writings which together form the Christian Old Testament and, with important variations, the Hebrew Bible, were composed over a long period, some nine hundred years. Their collection together as authoritative books for the community was also a lengthy process. In simple terms we may say that the earlier books of our Bibles were fixed first: the books of the Law and the historical books which record the story of Israel's entry into the Land and its subsequent glories and disasters. Next came the major prophetic books; and finally what were known as the "writings": psalms, songs, proverbs, and more meditative (and sometimes apparently skeptical) writings. It is often said that the Law was canonized around 400 BCE and the Prophets around 200 BCE. It is much less clear when the final section, the Writings, was fixed.

The New Testament, as we have seen, clearly recognizes the existence of authoritative scriptures (*graphai*) and it sometimes refers to these in more specific forms: "the law and the prophets" (Matthew 7:12; 22: 40; Luke 16:16; John 1:45; Acts 13:15, etc.). References to a further division of the scriptures, corresponding to the later threefold divisions into the Law, the Prophets, and the Writings, are hinted at in some of the later Jewish writings: the Preface to Sirach, Sirach 39:1–2, and 2 Maccabees

2:13–14. Luke 24:44 also refers to three divisions in a context which clearly implies that this refers to the whole of scripture, Jesus's appearance to the disciples after his resurrection at Emmaus: "Then he said to them, 'These are my words which I spoke to you, while I was still with you, that everything written about me in the law of Moses and the prophets and the psalms must be fulfilled.'"

The book of Isaiah is one of the major prophetic books of the Hebrew Bible. Several manuscripts of it were found among the Dead Sea Scrolls, the most complete being the Great Scroll of Isaiah, which comprises the book in its entirety. This portion of the Great Scroll of Isaiah contains Isaiah 34:1–37:24.

This impression of the relative fixity of the first two sections, the Law and the Prophets, and considerable fluidity where the third section is concerned is confirmed by the biblical manuscripts found among the Dead Sea Scrolls. Here we have nearly the entire contents (albeit in some cases in a very fragmentary state) of the library of a first-century Jewish sect. It contains all the books of the Hebrew Bible as now fixed, with the exception of the book of Esther. On the other hand, while this suggests that there was already a considerable consensus about the twenty-four books of scripture, there are other features which suggest a significant measure of fluidity at this period. In the first place, the copies of the Psalms found at Qumran contain some surprising omissions (thirty-five in all, including Psalm 110) and a considerable number of additions. The longest single scroll in Qumran, 11QPsa, contains forty-one psalms from the presently accepted Psalter, and a further eight not previously known in Hebrew. The library also contained a good number of writings (apart from those which were directly connected with the history and regulation of the life of the community itself) which are not contained in the present Hebrew Bible. Some of these were found in the Septuagint. Some (for example, the book of Jubilees, a retelling of the Genesis narrative, with theological ideas close to some of those found in the sect's own writings) remain outside the canons of either

The process of restoring and reconstructing the Dead Sea Scrolls was lengthy and painstaking. This photograph, taken in 1955 at the House of the Book in Jerusalem, shows a scholar working on some of the tiny, brittle fragments.

the Jewish or the Christian communities. Jubilees is however found in the Ethiopian canon.

It looks then as if it was some time after the Fall of Jerusalem in 70 CE, and the consequent removal of the Temple as a source of authority within Judaism, that the final shape of the Hebrew Bible emerged. This leaves interesting questions about the process of canonization. Who had authority to proclaim works canonical? Was it the group of Pharisees who, according to tradition, gathered around Johanan ben Zakkai at Jamnia (Yavneh) after the Fall of Jerusalem? Many now doubt that this grouping would have had the kind of authority required to command recognition throughout Jewish communities in the Mediterranean and the Middle East. It is likely that the process was more gradual, as communities came to recognize the value of some writings and the dangers of others. Those containing fierier visions of cosmic battles and the overthrow of Jewish enemies would have been regarded with caution in the light of the painful experiences of defeat at the hands of the Romans, not only in the Jewish War (66–73), but also in the Bar Kochba revolt in 132–35. The book of Enoch, which was in the Qumran library, was excluded, while others, like the book of Daniel, were retained, possibly because they had gained wider currency before the wars. Probably there was no firmly agreed canon until well into the second century CE.

Nor is this the end of the story. The text of the canonical writings at this point was written in unpointed Hebrew (and, in a few parts, Aramaic). This means that only the consonants were actually represented in the written texts. This leaves a good deal of room for scribal error and for different ways of vocalizing the consonants and indeed for regrouping consonants to give quite different words. It was only later that these ambiguities were in large measure resolved by the creation of a system of pointing the consonantal text to represent the missing vowels. This was the work of the Masoretes and the resulting text only began to be produced from the sixth century CE at the earliest.

The Greek Translation: The Septuagint

From the late fourth century BCE, after Alexander's successful campaigns, Greek became the principal means of communication for much of the world inhabited by Jews. There were Jewish communities living widely dispersed across the Mediterranean and the Middle East. Many Jews grew up in Greek-speaking cities like Alexandria and went to Greek schools. Many no longer spoke Hebrew. From the middle of the third century BCE translations into Greek began to be made of the Pentateuch, with the other books following over a period of centuries. That is to say, the process of translation into Greek was going on at the same time as the canon of the Hebrew Bible was being fixed.

The Greek translation is generally referred to as the Septuagint. This derives from the Latin *septuaginta*, meaning seventy, and the story in the Epistle of Aristeas that seventy-two elders translated the Pentateuch into Greek at the request of a King Ptolemy of Egypt. They were so well looked after and so industrious that they completed the task in seventy-two days. Although this story is generally regarded as legendary, the term has stuck, even in scholarly circles. The work is often referred to by the abbreviation LXX.

There are a number of intriguing features about this parallel process of translation and canonization. In the first place, there are substantial differences between the text of the Hebrew books and the Greek books, notably in the text of Jeremiah, which is much shorter in the Greek. (Interestingly, the Hebrew texts of Jeremiah found at Qumran are closer to the

Greek than to the canonical Hebrew text.) Secondly, there are substantial differences in the number of books included, both between different versions of the Septuagint and between the Septuagint and the Hebrew Bible. Generally speaking, 1 Esdras, Wisdom of Solomon, Sirach, Judith, Tobit, Baruch, the Letter of Jeremiah, 1–4 Maccabees, and the Psalms of Solomon are not found in the Hebrew Bible but are included in the Septuagint. Thirdly, there are variations in order. The threefold division of the Hebrew Bible is abandoned in the Septuagint. It appears that there was no clear division made between the Pentateuch and the rest of the historical books. Thereafter there is little agreement in the order of the books: some manuscripts place the psalms and wisdom literature before the prophets (as in Protestant Bibles), while others reverse this order. In some versions, the book of Daniel is included among the major prophets; in others it is among the minor ones.

The Christian Old Testament

While the Septuagint started life as a translation for Jews living in the Diaspora, it was subsequently taken up by the Christian community and became the medium through which the Old Testament (as it was now referred to) was known in the church. This meant that the Christian Bible from the start included more books than the equivalent Hebrew collections. The language of the Septuagint influenced many of the writers of the New Testament. It was not until St. Jerome translated the Christian Bible into Latin in the late fourth/early fifth century that the standing of the Septuagint was questioned. When Jerome started work there were already Latin translations of many of the books of the Bible. Jerome was concerned to get back to the original form of the Hebrew text, where that was available. He used an early form of the text of our present Hebrew

Saint Jerome (ca. 347–420), in response to a commission by Pope Damasus in 382, translated the Bible into Latin, a version known as the Vulgate—a condensation of the Latin phrase *versio vulgata,* or "common version." The Italian artist Vincenzo Catena (ca. 1470–1531) was one of many painters who depicted Jerome in his study, at work on his translation. Often appearing with Jerome are a lion, because Jerome is reputed to have once removed a thorn from a lion's paw, a quail, symbolic of truth, and a cardinal's hat.

Bible and went to considerable lengths to learn Hebrew. This introduced a strong element of stability into the text of the Christian Old Testament in its official Latin form, known as the Vulgate.

However, the history of the Christian Old Testament does not stop here by any means. The translation of the Bible into Latin marks the beginning of a parting of the ways between Western Latin-speaking Christianity and Eastern Christianity, which spoke Greek, Syriac, Coptic, Ethiopic, and other languages. The Bibles of the Eastern Churches vary considerably: the Ethiopic Orthodox canon includes eighty-one books and contains many apocalyptic texts, such as were found at Qumran and subsequently excluded from the Jewish canon. As a general rule, one can say that the Orthodox Churches generally follow the Septuagint in including more books in their Old Testaments than are in the Jewish canon.

The same was true of the West until the time of the Reformation. Here a sea change occurred. In the first place there was a renewal of interest in the Hebrew text of the Old Testament. The translators of the Authorized Version (or King James Version) of the Bible, criticizing the early Latin translations of the Old Testament, complain that "they were not out of

· · · · ·

The Authorized Version or King James Version of the Bible is probably the most famous of all the English translations of the Bible. It is certainly the one that has had most influence on English literature and language. It was commissioned by King James at the suggestion of John Reynolds, the leader of the English Puritans, at the Hampton Court Conference of 1604. Some fifty scholars, working in six groups, set to work in Cambridge, Oxford, and Westminster to compare and revise existing translations in order to produce a standard version for use in the Church of England. The first edition appeared in 1611 and there have been a number of subsequent small amendments. Until 1988, when it lost its position to the New International Version, it was the best-selling Bible in the United States.

· · · · ·

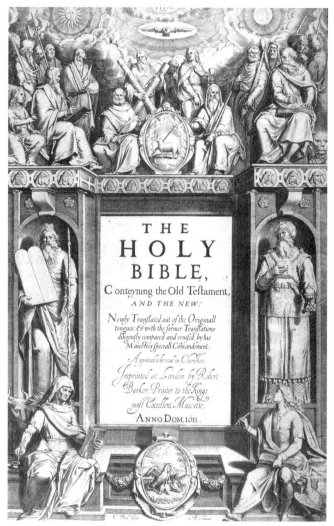

This frontispiece to a 1611 edition of the King James Bible portrays Matthew, Mark, Luke, and John—the four Evangelists—in the four corners, each accompanied by his symbolic creature. The twelve apostles stand at the top of the page; Moses and Aaron flank the text in the center panel.

the Hebrew fountain, . . . but out of the Greek stream; therefore the Greek being not altogether clear, the Latin derived from it must needs be muddy." Jerome by contrast translated "out of the very fountains themselves."

Allied with this, though not explicitly set out in the Authorized Version Preface, goes a much greater respect for the books of the Hebrew Bible than for those found only in the Septuagint. These books are clearly separated from the books of the Old and New Testaments and referred to as "The books called Apocrypha." The expression "apocrypha," a plural noun from the Greek adjective meaning "hidden" or "obscure," was introduced by the German Reformer Carlstadt in 1520. The suggestion is that these books are to be reserved for the wise or initiated. The Reformers regarded them with suspicion because the Second Book of Maccabees included prayers for the dead (2 Maccabees 12:43–44), a Catholic practice rejected by them. This general mistrust is reflected in the lectionaries which are found in the Anglican Book of Common Prayer, where only rarely are passages to be publicly read from the Apocrypha, and then mostly from Ecclesiasticus (ben Sirach) or Baruch or the Wisdom of Solomon. The Roman Catholic Church, by contrast, reaffirmed the authority of these books, referring to them as "deuterocanonical," that is, secondarily canonical. The version of the Vulgate published after the Council of Trent redistributed them among the books of the Old Testament (as in the Septuagint), but relegated the Prayer of Manasseh and 3 and 4 Ezra to an appendix. In a further twist to the story, from the 1820s onward it became a widespread practice among (Protestant) Bible societies to print Bibles without the Apocrypha at all. More recent ecumenical editions of the Bible, like the Common Bible, have restored the Apocrypha or deuterocanonical books.

· · · · ·

The Council of Trent (1545–63) was convened by Pope Paul III at the instigation of the Holy Roman Emperor Charles V to attempt to resolve the disputes of the Reformation period and to reform ecclesiastical abuses within the Catholic Church. In practice it served to define Catholic doctrinal responses to the teachings of the Reformers and to resolve doctrinal issues which had been previously open. It gave rulings on, among many other subjects, the relation of scripture and tradition, the nature of biblical inspiration, and the place of the *magisterium* (the teaching office of the Catholic Church) in the interpretation of the Bible. It issued authoritative lists of the canonical and deuterocanonical books of the Bible and authorized the Vulgate as the official Latin translation of the Bible for church use.

· · · · ·

The Christian New Testament

The process of the formation of the Christian canon of the New Testament (that is, of writings which have a specifically Christian origin) is not all that dissimilar from that by which the Hebrew scriptures came to be canonized.

In the early days of Christianity, there were of course no scriptures written by Christians. "Scripture" for the early Christians was what they would subsequently come to call the scriptures of the Old Testament. Nor is it likely that the first Christian writings were composed as scripture. Once, however, Christian writings began to be seen as scripture themselves, there was a need to distinguish them from the older writings. The terms "old testament" and "new testament" come into currency at the end of the second century. Originally they referred respectively to the

In 1588, the artist Pasquale Cati painted this depiction of the Council of Trent. Note the allegorical figure of the Church Triumphant in the foreground, portrayed as a woman with a papal tiara.

covenants which God had made with the people of Israel through Moses and with the church through Jesus. The sense was that these were books belonging to the old or new covenant, not that the books themselves were the covenants. Later of course the terms came to refer to the books themselves, as on the title page of the King James Bible: "The Holy Bible conteyning the Old Testament, and the New" (see page 56).

How did the Christian writings of the founding figures come to be recognized as authoritative for the church? The purposes of the books are varied: Paul's letters were occasional communications to churches around the Mediterranean (or exceptionally to an individual, Philemon), addressing specific matters of belief and practice. They were in some ways a substitute for his own presence, offering advice, exhortation, argument, admonition, scolding. They were undoubtedly intended as an exercise of authority on Paul's part and were probably intended to be read out at meetings of the congregation. In this sense they had, from the start, a function in the worship of the communities to which they were addressed. Some of the other letters, notably the so-called Catholic epistles (James, 1 and 2 Peter, 1–3 John), may have been intended for wider circulation, as indeed was the Book of Revelation, though this is strictly an apocalypse (an account of visions and revelations) rather than a letter.

It is rather more difficult to say what the purpose or purposes behind the writing of the Gospels were. Some have thought that they, like Paul's letters, were written to address particular issues within their own communities. Matthew's Gospel, it has been suggested, was written in the aftermath of the destruction of the Temple to legitimize the position of his Christian Jewish congregation in relation to the dominant Jewish group, the heirs to the Pharisaic tradition. Thus Jesus is presented as a teacher who "fulfills the Law and the prophets" (5:17) and the Pharisees are attacked as "blind guides" (15:14). On the other hand, we must not overlook the obvious, which is that the evangelists were principally writing down a record of the life, death, and resurrection of Jesus. In so doing they were recording for posterity, and importantly giving their own view of, the events on which their faith was centered. It is unlikely that they would have undertaken such a labor simply for a small congregation in one particular settlement. Certainly such works quickly gained a wider circulation, and there were soon many more in circulation than the four which we now know from the New Testament. Such writings will certainly have been regarded as scripture before ever the question was

The epistles of the apostle Paul, who is portrayed in this ca. 1470 portrait by the artist Marco Zoppo, were the first early Christian texts to be collected. They were included in the early lists of canonical New Testament books.

resolved of which ones should be included in the authoritative list of Christian scriptures.

That is to say, there was a growing number of Christian writings in circulation in the churches scattered around the Mediterranean which, whatever their original intention and occasion, came to be regarded as in some sense scriptural. How did the canon of the New Testament come to be fixed? Scholars disagree on this, and what follows is only one view. The problem is that the evidence for the process is scattered and often indirect. Scholars have to rely on evidence of the use of the various New Testament books by theologians during the period from the second to the fifth centuries, as well as on the various ecclesiastical rulings on the authority or orthodoxy of particular books which might be included in the canon, and on the actual contents of particular manuscripts. All of this has to be evaluated against the general picture of the development of the early church which historians have built up.

The first stage in the formation of the canon was the making of collections of Christian writings. Paul's letters were the earliest writings to be collected together, some time at the beginning of the second century. The earliest collection has ten letters (1 and 2 Corinthians, Romans, Ephesians, 1 and 2 Thessalonians, Galatians, Philippians, Colossians, Philemon). Later versions add the so-called Pastoral Epistles: 1 and 2 Timothy and Titus. Eventually the Epistle to the Hebrews (which, unlike the others, does not contain an opening address by Paul to the recipients) was also added to the collection. This collection was not initially much cited, but by the end of the second century it enjoyed widespread respect and use among the church leaders, despite the fact that it had been the main source of doctrine of one of the earliest "heretics," Marcion.

· · · · ·

PSEUDONYMITY IN THE BIBLE

In the ancient world writings were often attributed to well-known authors and figures, when in fact they were written by someone else. In Greek literature, there are writings falsely attributed to Plato and Socrates. In the Old Testament, psalms are attributed to David, although they were certainly not all written by him. Many of the laws attributed to Moses come from a later period of royal legislation; wisdom material is attributed to Solomon; substantial additions of later prophetic material are made to the books of Isaiah and Zechariah. There is a whole class of so-called Pseudepigrapha—writings, dating from the turn of the era, acknowledged by the church to have false attributions (such as Jubilees, which is said to have been written by Moses, even though it is a retelling of parts of Genesis).

The extent to which the New Testament contains pseudonymous writings is a more contentious issue. Were all the letters credited to Paul actually written by him? Colossians and Ephesians certainly contain language and thought which is unlike that of Romans and Galatians, but there are strong similarities too. The Pastoral Epistles seem to flatten Paul's thought and to be more concerned with church order and respectability than with the power of the gospel. Many scholars doubt that the Gospels were written by eyewitnesses as their attributions seem to suggest: there is too much evidence of reworking oral traditions and of straight borrowing from other Gospels to make this likely.

Why would people who were concerned with the truth have deliberately falsified the authorship of their works? No single explanation will do. In some cases, an ancient authority may be appealed to to give radical views the force of tradition. The visions of 1 and 2 Enoch may fit this account. In other cases writers in a particular school may have felt themselves so indebted to the ideas of their master that they continued to write under his name. In so doing they may also have on occasion wished to defend him from subsequent attacks. This may explain how some of the letters in the New Testament came to be attributed to Paul.

· · · · ·

The next collection to emerge was the fourfold Gospel. This was a more contentious matter. The four canonical writings were probably all written by the end of the first century, but that was by no means the end of the writing of Gospels. This overproduction of good news, while understandable, given that different groups were keen to promote their understanding of the tradition, nevertheless caused problems for the ordinary reader, who could easily be confused by such diversity in fundamental matters of the faith. In 170 Tatian sought to find a solution by composing a single narrative out of Matthew, Mark, and Luke, with some additional oral material. Nevertheless such attempts at harmonization were ultimately unsuccessful. By the end of the second century a "fourfold gospel" had come to be accepted. It contained four books, each of which told "the" gospel according to the perspective of the particular evangelist. This is itself a remarkable feature, enshrining a political compromise at the heart of the Christian canon: no one contender, not even a hybrid, could command overwhelming support. Behind this compromise one might discern a wider perception that no one

After Paul's epistles, the four Gospels were the next texts to be canonized. The Codex purpureus Rossanensis (also known as the Rossano Gospels), a sixth-century manuscript believed to have originated in Aleppo, Syria, contains the gospel of Matthew and almost the entire gospel of Mark. This folio from the codex depicts Christ's entry into Jerusalem.

account could be adequate to express the one gospel to which all four witness. This understanding is reflected in the titles given to the Gospels: "the Gospel according to Matthew," etc. The Gospels are attempts, from their different standpoints, to express the mystery of what has been revealed to the church.

· · · · ·

The process by which Gospels were accepted as canonical is not easy to define. At one level, what was important was that they were read publicly in the services of the main churches. There is clear evidence that the four canonical Gospels were well established by the end of the second century, even though there had been reservations about the fourth Gospel (John) because of its attractiveness to Gnostic (heretical) circles. Other Gospels like the Gospel of Thomas (actually a collection of sayings of Jesus), the Gospels according to the Hebrews, of the Ebionites, according to the Egyptians, of Philip, of Matthias, of Peter were more closely associated with Jewish Christian or Gnostic groupings which were marginal to the main body of the church and did not gain the same measure of acceptance.

· · · · ·

While these two collections were fixed by the end of the second century, there was less agreement about the contents of the third major section which would be included in the New Testament canon: the Catholic epistles. These were letters which were held to have been written to all the churches, rather than to a particular congregation. Generally, though not universally, 1 Peter and 1 John were accepted as canonical in the second and third centuries. Other writings took longer to be accepted: James, 2 Peter (a late work), 2 and 3 John (very polemical writings, *inter alia* forbidding believers even to greet those who are considered deviant to the group), and Jude had much less support. 2 and 3 John were still rejected in parts of the East as late as the sixth century.

It appears then that the process of acceptance of Christian writings by the churches was a gradual one, closely connected with the formation of such collections. In the fourth century a number of lists of canonical writings were made, which in differing measure contain much of what is in the present canon and a certain amount that is not. There are also significant variations, especially in regard to 2 Peter, 2 and 3 John, Hebrews, Jude, and Revelation.

Eusebius, bishop of Caesarea (ca. 265–340; see page 31), depicted in this 1584 French engraving, wrote several books analyzing biblical texts, including *Demonstration of the Gospel, Preparation for the Gospel,* and *On Discrepancies Between the Gospels.*

· · · · ·

EARLY CHURCH LISTS OF THE BOOKS OF THE NEW TESTAMENT

The numbers in parentheses give totals. The lists indicate the considerable divergence of view about the canonical status of some books during the first centuries.

Muratorian Canon (24)
Four Gospels
Acts
13 letters of Paul
   (i.e., not Hebrews)
Jude
1 and 2 John
Wisdom of Solomon
Revelation
Apocalypse of Peter

Codex Claromontanus (27)
Four Gospels
10 letters of Paul
   (not Philippians, 1 and
   2 Thessalonians)
1 and 2 Peter
James
1, 2, 3 John
Jude
Epistle of Barnabas
Revelation of John
Acts of the Apostles
Acts of Paul
Shepherd of Hermas
Apocalypse of Peter

Eusebius

Accepted (21 or 22)
Four Gospels
Acts
14 letters of Paul
1 Peter
1 John
Revelation (?)

Disputed (9 or 10)
James
Jude
2 Peter
2 and 3 John
Acts of Paul
Shepherd of Hermas
Apocalypse of Peter
Didache
Revelation (?)

Rejected
Gospels of Peter, Thomas,
   and Matthias, etc.
Acts of Andrew, John, etc.

· · · · ·

This long process of acceptance of texts as canonical was eventually concluded by a series of decisions of church councils, though none of these councils was a general (ecumenical) council of the church. Even so there was still disagreement. The Council of Laodicaea (363) omitted Revelation from the list; the Councils of Hippo (393) and Carthage (397) gave the present list of twenty-seven books. As a general rule, books were included which were judged to have been written by one of the apostles, to have been addressed to the church at large (meeting the criterion of catholicity) and from the early times, and which were believed to be orthodox. These criteria were, however, applied flexibly: there were doubts about the apostolic authorship of Hebrews; the Pauline epistles were not strictly catholic; Jude and 2 Peter had not enjoyed a long tradition of use. Revelation was questioned, partly because it had been popular among heretical groups (such as the Montanists), partly because there were those who claimed that its promises would be fulfilled in an earthly reign of Christ, a view easily associated with political unrest and subversion. Its apostolic authorship was attacked and it was not accepted in the East until the tenth/eleventh centuries.

What's the Use of a Canon?

We have just had a very brief look at how the different collections of books were made by different faith communities and had sacred and normative status conferred on them. We saw how, in both Jewish and Christian communities, this process was for the most part informal: different collections of books came to be recognized as sacred, authoritative, particularly appropriate for use in worship. To use the language of later Christian theology, the process of reception of the canon preceded that of formal definition. Moreover, this process of recognition was often a contentious one. It was not only a question of certain collections gradually gaining popularity. There were also books whose position within a collection, or within the final authorized collection, was contentious. People wanted to fight not only for the inclusion but also for the exclusion of certain works. In the East the book of Revelation, with its millenarian fervor, was regarded with great suspicion. Such books were subversive and only to be treated with great caution and interpretive skill.

That is to say, the process of canonization of scripture is a process of conferring authority on some books and of refusing to confer authority on others. Sacred books carry a charge which has to be carefully controlled: they are a source of power and life for the communities which use them, but they are also potentially threatening. The communities which live by them may also grow apart by them. The same scriptures which have sustained a community through its history may suddenly be turned against it and cause painful and violent rifts.

What sort of authority is canonical authority as applied to writings? Moshe Halberthal, a Jewish philosopher teaching in Jerusalem, has helpfully distinguished different types of authority which may be attributed to texts: normative and formative. Such authority may be normative: to recognize certain texts as canonical may be to declare that they contain (or generate) norms which regulate the lives of the communities which accept them. They provide the means for the community to make decisions, to manage conflicts, and to give rulings in matters of belief and practice. Law codes are perhaps the best example of such texts. Declaring the Bible to be canonical is on this view to declare that it can all be read as a source of rulings on faith and practice for the church. Practices which are described in the Bible may then be regarded as prescribing (or at the least as sanctioning), certain forms of action: for example, prayers for the dead (2 Maccabees 12:43–44) or the extermination of indigenous peoples (Joshua, Judges, 1 Samuel 15). But while the Bible certainly contains legal codes, it contains a good deal more: narrative, proverbial material, poetry, letters, lives of Jesus.

But this is not the only way that canonical writings function in the communities which accept them. Literary classics which form the basis of educational curricula in certain countries may have no normative, legal force, but they still have a very powerful formative role in the communities which accept them. The classical literature of ancient Greece, "the Bible and Shakespeare," Goethe and Schiller, and other classics have variously provided communities in Europe and North America with a common language and thought which enables them to discourse about and to make sense of their experience. Communities shaped by such a body of writings will tend to share certain basic beliefs about the world and the proper ways to behave in this world, which will both strongly bond them together and also provide the means of conducting fierce debates about these common beliefs. In practice, the biblical scriptures have exercised such a formative role, every bit as much as being drawn on as a source of rules and norms for the life and faith of the community. They have provided ordinary believers—and indeed those with no particularly strong beliefs—with conceptual tools to make sense of their lives, which they have done in many different ways. For many this has not been the stuff of controversy. For others these different uses of biblical language and imagery to make sense of experience have generated fierce debate and conflict. The Jews who lived at Qumran lived out of the same scriptures as other contemporary Jews; they shared with them basic beliefs about the Temple, the Land, the Law, and the covenant, but they disagreed strongly about the detailed interpretation of these beliefs. The Christian Reformers of the sixteenth century shared many of the same beliefs as the Popes and priests of the Catholic Church with whom they so strongly disagreed, beliefs which were supported and "proved" by scripture. But they also used scripture to provide powerful arguments against certain tenets of the medieval church. When Luther finally grasped the sense of the expression "the righteousness of God" on which he was to found the Reformation, he said that it was as if the gates of paradise had been opened to him: a whole new way of reading scripture, and therefore of conceiving the world and human action and behavior, flowed from this breakthrough. The fact that first-century

· · · · ·

The desire to resolve the fierce religious conflicts of the sixteenth century by authoritative appeal to a normative Bible is well reflected in Valerianus Magni's work: *An assessment of the rule of believing of non-Catholics.* Magni was a Capuchin monk who was active in converting Protestants after the Reformation, and who also fell foul of the Jesuits. In his book he seeks to establish a rule for reading scripture which will lead to complete agreement in matters of faith. Properly understood, scripture will determine correct belief with mathematical certainty:

> A rule is an instrument with the aid of which lines which one draws necessarily come out straight; accordingly that norm which those who follow do not err in believing is called the rule of believing.

Quoted in Scholder, p. 14

· · · · ·

Jews and sixteenth-century Reformers and Catholics then appealed to scripture as normative, as a means of providing authoritative rulings in such debates, only aggravated the conflict.

However, in most cases the relationship between the canonical biblical texts and the meanings that people take from them is even more complicated than that between legal codes and legal rulings. In the first place, as we have been noticing, the texts themselves are complex and diverse. They are the product of a long process of composition and compilation. They are by no means always unambiguous. There are passages whose meaning is less than clear, others which are straightforwardly ambiguous. Moreover, some of the texts are, by their very nature as metaphorical or poetic, intended to prompt people to re-envision their own world in their light, rather than simply to prescribe a way of looking at it. In all such cases the role of readers will not be simply to construe the meaning of the texts. They will rather read them in such a way as to illuminate their own beliefs and experience of the world.

Including a text within one's canon of scripture gives it authoritative status within the community. But what if it is apparently at odds with the community's beliefs and expectations? The Song of Songs is a wonderful love song: but what can be made of such a poem as sacred scripture? The outlook of the Book of Ecclesiastes is profoundly skeptical: what is to be made of a book which appears to deny outright that there is any connection between virtue and vice and rewards and punishments? In such cases interpretative strategies may need to be found to reduce the dissonances and to bring harmony into the discord of the sacred writings. Their meaning, as Halberthal somewhat provocatively puts it, is changed by virtue of their inclusion in the canon of scripture. If they are here, then they must have an appropriate meaning.

There is a further sense in which their inclusion in the canon can cause problems for texts. By virtue of such inclusion, the community lays claim to them; it claims too to know how to read and interpret them (however much such reading strategies may vary in the course of time). If they are the canonical texts of this community, which upholds this worldview and this ethos, then they must broadly be read from such a perspective. But such claims will provoke opposition from those outside

The Song of Solomon, or Song of Songs, as it is referred to in the opening verse, falls into the category of Wisdom Books, along with (among others) Job, Psalms, and Ecclesiastes. Despite its vividly erotic character, it occurs in all the major versions of the Bible, the Hebrew Bible, the Greek Old Testament, and the Western and Eastern Christian Old Testaments. This illuminated initial *O* from the twelfth-century Winchester Bible begins Song of Solomon 1:2: "Osculetur me osculo oris sui quia meliora sunt ubera tua vino" (Let him kiss me with the kisses of his mouth: for thy breasts are better than wine).

the community of faith. They may wish to reclaim them and to read them in ways which may be in strong contrast to those of the community of faith; or they may accept such readings as giving the sense of scripture and then seek to attack them. The very power of sacred texts may generate sustained and heated debates between believers and religion's "cultured despisers," as Schleiermacher, one of the founders of modern theology, termed them.

What we shall attempt to do in the rest of this book is to look at some of the ways in which the biblical texts have been read both by believers and those outside the various faith communities which have lived out of some form of the Bible. This will be in large measure a descriptive exercise: I hope that the sheer variety of readings associated with these texts will provoke a certain respect. For some, such respect may be coupled with affection, even love. For others, it may be more like the respect one accords to an unexploded bomb. It is not hard to see why such different reactions are both possible and appropriate.

FOUR

The Bible in the World
of the Believers

●

TEXTS, ONCE CANONIZED, CHANGE. They become sacred texts. In the communities which recognize their new status, believers regard them as set apart, special texts to be treated like no other texts. For this reason, their expectations about these texts are rather different from those which they have of other texts. Precisely because the canonical texts are sacred, it is unthinkable that they should conflict with believers' own deepest sense of the sacred. Any serious dissonance between the community's experience and the world of the sacred text cries out for resolution. Either the world of the text must be made to conform to the experience of the community, or the community must change to conform with the text.

For many—if not most—communities of Christian believers, the Bible serves as a touchstone of faith. This 1954 photograph shows members of a United Brethren in Christ congregation consulting their Bibles.

A powerful dialectic is set up. Believers read the texts in the light of their own experience; and, at the same time, they look to the texts to make sense of and to shape their experience. We should then expect that different communities of believers will read the same text in very different ways. In this we will find a reflection both of their different beliefs and their different histories.

This is not altogether different from what happens with classical, non-sacred texts, but the intensity of the reactions is different. If Shakespeare and Goethe come to be regarded as classics for respectable bourgeois society, then there will be those who wish to screen out certain aspects of their writings which they regard as shocking, even simply as impolite. Anthologies of Goethe will omit some of his more unbuttoned love poetry; Bowdler produces his sanitized versions of Shakespeare. The comparison is instructive: such conflicts between literary and aesthetic works and respectable taste and sensibilities mostly create only a temporary scandal; they rarely lead to lasting splits in a community. They may lead to changes in sensibility. There is a recognition that writers and artists may help people to come to terms with the heights and depths of experience which polite society simply ignores or suppresses. Such changes in sensibility also occur, as we shall see, in religious communities. Sometimes they encounter much greater resistance, as communities fight to defend ways of looking at the world which are sanctified by traditional readings of scripture.

Let us consider a single text which has had profound resonances in both the Jewish and Christian traditions and look at some of the ways in which it has shaped and been shaped by the very different experiences of these two families of communities.

Regardless of the persuasiveness of this or any particular interpretation, that conviction lies at the heart of Midrash all the time: the Scriptures are not only a record of the past but a prophecy, a foreshadowing and foretelling, of what will come to pass. And if that is the case, text and personal experience are not two autonomous domains. On the contrary, they are reciprocally enlightening: even as the immediate event helps make the age-old sacred text intelligible, so in turn the text reveals the fundamental significance of the recent event or experience.

Judah Goldin (The Last Trial, p. xx)

The Akedah

The Akedah, the story of Abraham's binding of Isaac in Genesis 22 touches a deep nerve in Jewish and Christian sensibilities. It is a story of strange violence and tenderness, of a father ordered by his God to sacrifice "his only son." Only at the last moment are Abraham and Isaac rescued from the approaching horror by the intervention of an angel. The story is told with all the power and economy and concreteness of Biblical narrative at its best. Abraham and Isaac leave the servants behind and set off: "And Abraham took the wood of the burnt offering, and laid it on Isaac his son; and he took in his hand the fire and the knife. So they went both of them together" (Genesis 22:6). That last sentence, repeated two verses later, and the ensuing short dialogue emphasize the bonds between the two; yet Abraham's obedience to God drives them on to the mountain of sacrifice. There he stretches out his hand and takes up the knife to kill his son. Only then does the angel intervene. Yet out of the near disaster comes blessing and the promise of a new nation which shall spring from the father and his son. The range of emotions and experiences which is embraced in this short, tersely written narrative is remarkable, and this is reflected in the richness of its subsequent readings.

One of the earliest interpretations of the story is found in the Book of Jubilees. The author has the major section of the work narrated to Moses by the angel of the presence. This enables him to fill in the heavenly background to the story, which is missing in the biblical narrative. We are now told why it was that God tested Abraham (Genesis 22:1). Reports had been circulating in heaven about Abraham's faithfulness and love of God. This had in turn prompted Satan, whose name is given as Prince Mastema, to challenge the genuineness of Abraham's love for God, asserting that Abraham loved his son Isaac more. The angel says that God knew that Abraham's love was genuine, for he had already tested him many times, but nevertheless he prepares one final trial for Abraham. This theme of the last trial will run on through Jewish discussions of the story.

The motif of Abraham's trial is already found in Genesis, but in Jubilees there is a subtle yet significant shift of emphasis. The trial is not a means of God finding out whether Abraham loves and obeys him. Here God (and the reader) knows this from the start, and at the crucial moment God intervenes because of this knowledge. In Genesis by contrast it is only after Abraham has taken the knife that God, through the angel, says "for now I know that you fear God, seeing that you have not withheld your son, your only son, from me" (Genesis 22:12). In Jubilees the purpose of God's action is to demonstrate to Mastema Abraham's faithfulness and love of God. This is clear from God's final words to Abraham: "And I have made known to all that you are faithful to me in everything which I say to you."

• • • • •

The Book of Jubilees is for the most part a retelling of Genesis and the early chapters of Exodus, with omissions, condensations, explanations, and insertions. The book is prefaced by God's telling Moses of Israel's future apostasy and ultimate restoration. Its origin in the second century BCE suggests that the writer is reflecting on the terrible events of the proscription of Judaism by the Seleucid king Antiochus Epiphanes. A contemporary source tells of one mother who encouraged seven of her sons to die rather than apostatize, and then met a martyr's death herself (2 Maccabees 7). The Jews, however, rose up and eventually a new Jewish monarchy was established, which enjoyed a century of relative independence before falling under Roman control.

Antiochus IV Epiphanes (ca. 215–164 BCE) outlawed Judaism throughout his empire; his persecutions led to the Maccabean Revolt (167 BCE), which initiated a long, drawn-out military struggle that in turn led to the establishment of the Hasmonaean dynasty. This marble head of Antiochus was created some time around 170 BCE.

• • • • •

This becomes a message to the Jews, who have just themselves undergone such Satanic testing. The purpose of Abraham's and, by extension, their own trials is to make Israel's faithfulness to God known, so that "all the nations may bless themselves" by them (Jubilees 18:16).

The introduction of Satan adds a further dimension to the story, alongside the motif of God's testing of Abraham's obedience. There are

Philo of Alexandria (20 BCE–50 CE), depicted in this sixteenth-century engraving, was one of the greatest of Jewish philosophers and commentators on the Bible. Like many scholars, he wrote about the Akedah, or Abraham's binding of Isaac to a sacrificial altar.

now seen to be dark powers in the world who lead people astray and who wish to claim even the most righteous as their victims. In a rather obscure way, some of the responsibility for human suffering falls upon Satan, while God and his angels are portrayed as being there to support and protect the faithful. In the story, they are there, ensuring that no harm comes to Isaac (at least no physical harm). But how does this chime in with the experiences of Jews down the ages of persecution and martyrdom, which brought many to their death?

Awareness of these problems is to be found in the first-century Jewish writer Philo of Alexandria. Philo's community in Alexandria was at the receiving end of discrimination and persecution. In his treatise *De Abrahamo*, he deals first with accusations that Abraham's trial was of no great account compared with those pagans who had willingly sacrificed offspring for the preservation of their cities or people. But, says Philo, for Abraham, for whom human sacrifice was abominable, sacrificing his son would have been an even more terrible trial. For pagan princes, such a thing would have been almost second nature (*De Abrahamo,* 177–99). Philo's treatment does not stop there. He also wants to make a point about human suffering and affliction, which he does by bringing out the allegorical significance of the story. Isaac's name means laughter. Abraham sacrifices laughter, or rather "the good emotion of the understanding, that is joy" out of a sense of duty to God. This is proper because a life of pure joy and happiness is for God alone. Nevertheless, God will allow those who are faithful to share a measure of such joy, though even so it will be admixed with sorrow (*De Abrahamo,* 200–7). One is reminded of the Jewish joke: Why don't Jews get drunk? Because when you drink, you forget your troubles.

But what of the greater sufferings of Jews themselves? The terrible persecution inflicted on Jews at the time of Antiochus Epiphanes (175 BCE) produced its own tales of Jewish faithfulness to God under extreme torture. One of these (in 2 Maccabees 7) tells of a mother who witnesses—and encourages—the gruesome martyrdom of her seven sons, before she herself too is killed. In a later rabbinic retelling, the story is transposed from its original setting in the time of Antiochus Epiphanes to the second century CE, when Jews were persecuted under the Roman Emperor Hadrian. The story is full both of the pain of such suffering and of pride in the martyrs for their faith. "The mother wept and said [to her sons]: Children, do not be distressed, for to this end were you created—to sanctify in the world the Name of the Holy One, blessed be He. Go and tell Father Abraham: Let not your heart swell with pride! You built one altar, but I have built seven altars and on them have offered up my seven sons. What is more: Yours was a trial; mine was an accomplished fact!" (Yalkut, Deuteronomy 26, 938).

An even more anguished response to the story comes in the medieval retellings during the persecutions of the Jews at the time of the Crusades. The Jewish chronicles of the time record how, when the Crusaders attacked, Jews, rather than risk forced conversion under torture, would offer each other up as a sacrifice, inspecting the knife for blemishes that might render the sacrifice invalid, and reciting an appropriate blessing. The synagogue poetry of the time compares such sacrifices with the Akedah of Isaac:

The martyrdom of the seven Maccabean brothers and their mother is depicted in this fresco from the Pfarrkirche Sankt Pankratius (Saint Pancras church) in Wiggensbach, Germany, painted by the artist Franz Joseph Hermann in 1771.

O Lord, Mighty One, dwelling on high!

Once, over one Akedah, Ariels cried out before Thee,

But now how many are butchered and burned!

Why over the blood of children did they not raise a cry?

Before that patriarch could in his haste sacrifice his only one,

It was heard from heaven: Do not put forth your hand to destroy!

But how many sons and daughters of Judah are slain—

While yet He makes no haste to save those butchered nor those cast
on the flames.

> Fragment from a Threnody *by R. Eliezer bar Joel ha-Levi in Spiegel, pp. 20–21*

Or again:

On the merit of the Akedah at Moriah once we could lean, Safeguarded
for the salvation of age after age—

Now one Akedah follows another, they cannot be counted.

> *R. David bar Meshullam*, Selihot, *49, 66b, in Spiegel, p. 21*

But the most remarkable treatment of the Akedah story from this period comes from the pen of R. Ephraim ben Jacob of Bonn, for here we read that Abraham not only actually carried out the ritual slaughter of his son, but that, when God immediately brought Isaac back to life, he attempted to repeat the sacrifice.

He [Abraham] made haste, he pinned him [Isaac] down with his knees,

He made his two arms strong,

With steady hands he slaughtered him according to the rite,

Full right was the slaughter.

Down upon him fell the resurrecting dew, and he revived

(The father) seized him (then) to slaughter him once more.

Scripture bear witness! Well-grounded is the fact:

And the Lord called Abraham, even a second time from heaven.

Spiegel, pp. 148–49

Remarkably, the poet claims scriptural support for his account of Abraham's attempt to sacrifice his son a second time. In the Genesis story, it is true, the angel calls Abraham twice, once to stop the sacrifice, once to give Abraham the promise that he will be the father of a great nation. R. Ephraim gives a very different rendering of the two calls. Abraham evidently fails to hear, or ignores, the first. Spiegel, in his deeply sympathetic account of this poem, comments tersely on the phrase "well-grounded is the fact": "If not in Scripture, then in the experience of the Jews in the Middle Ages" (p. 138). The terrible experiences of Jews in the persecutions of the Middle Ages must find an echo in their sacred texts.

Christian interpretation of the Akedah, by contrast, is refracted through its own central narrative of the crucifixion of Jesus. Remarkably though, despite the obvious similarities between the two stories, there are few actual literary allusions to the Akedah in the Gospel narratives. When Jesus prays to God in the Garden of Gethsemane on the night before his crucifixion, we may hear distant echoes of Isaac's questioning of his father and the subsequent traditions of his willing acceptance of his father's purpose. Of course the plot is different: there is no human father as mediator of God's purposes; no relenting on the part of the heavenly father; no mere testing of the victim's father.

Rather it is the victim himself who must struggle to accept freely the heavenly Father's unwavering will (a motif which does indeed occur in some of the versions of the Akedah). Is it too much to see some of these points reflected in the Gospel retellings of Jesus's prayer in the Garden (see below)?

· · · · ·

THE SON'S ACCEPTANCE OF THE FATHER'S WILL

In Mark, Matthew, and Luke, Jesus finally accepts his coming death in the Garden of Gethsemane after the Last Supper. In John this scene is set earlier, after the entry into Jerusalem. Here Jesus's words are spoken publicly before the crowds and are met with an approving voice from heaven. John, however, picks up the theme of the cup in his account of Jesus's arrest.

Mark 14:36

Abba, Father, all things are possible to thee; remove this cup from me; yet not what I will, but what thou wilt.

Matthew 26:39

And going a little farther he fell on his face and prayed, "My Father, if it be possible, let this cup pass from me; nevertheless, not as I will, but as thou wilt."

Luke 22:42

Father, if thou art willing, remove this cup from me; nevertheless not my will, but thine, be done.

John 12:27

"Now is my soul troubled. And what shall I say? 'Father, save me from this hour'? No, for this purpose I have come to this hour. Father, glorify thy name." Then a voice came from heaven. "I have glorified it, and I will glorify it again."

John 18:11

Jesus said to Peter, "Put your sword into its sheath; shall I not drink the cup which the Father has given me?"

· · · · ·

Matthew and Luke somehow stumble over Mark's bald "all things are possible to you," a traditional ascription of omnipotence. Matthew, faced with the enormity of God's killing his own son, seems to raise the question whether there is not some higher necessity controlling the action. Luke seems more concerned with the question of the unity or constancy of the divine will: how can the Son of God pray to God in order to change his mind? John omits the whole episode of Jesus's prayer in the garden, replacing it with a comparable scene of anguish immediately before the Last Supper (12:27). He makes this a more public scene at which not only Jews but Greeks are present. Jesus's acceptance of his mission will glorify the divine name, just as Abraham's obedience had done before. This acceptance is echoed in Jesus's remark to Peter at his arrest (18:11). All that is left now is Jesus's affirmation of his complete acceptance of his Father's will: had he not said earlier "My food is to do the will of the one who sent me" (John 4:34)?

In all this, the Father's will does not waver. Only at one point is this emphasis on the relentlessness of the Father's will qualified: in the evangelists' vivid portrayal of the human actors who conspire to bring about Jesus's death. Mark's account of Jesus's arrest is introduced by Jesus's own words: "It is enough; the hour has come; the Son of Man is delivered into the hands of sinners. Rise, let us be going; see, he who will deliver me is at hand" (Mark 14:41–42). There is an ambiguity

The Gospels of Matthew, Mark, and Luke recount the story of Jesus's night prayer in the Garden of Gethsemane. Andrea Mantegna's ca. 1460 painting *Agony in the Garden* depicts Jesus kneeling on a rock, accompanied by three disciples—Peter, James, and John—who sleep despite Jesus's admonition to stay awake, an element in the story that Luke omits.

here in the use of the word "deliver." It means both simply "hand over" and also "betray." Does it refer only to Judas's betraying him to the band sent out by the chief priests? Or does it not also suggest the divine agency behind the events which now overwhelm Jesus, handing him over into the hands of his destroyers? (The same—Greek—word occurs in Isaiah 53:6: "the Lord has delivered on to [laid on] him our transgressions.") Probably this ambiguity is intentional, but in the ensuing narrative it is the violent action of the arresting mob which is emphasized with four occurrences of the verb "seize" in the account and two references to the mob's "swords and clubs." Jesus is caught up in the chief priests' and scribes' plans to kill him and they, after a perfunctory trial, "bind him" and "deliver" him to Pilate.

It is tempting to see here an inversion of the themes in the Genesis narrative. There Abraham takes Isaac, binds him, and offers him up to God in obedience to God's command. Here it is sinners who seize Jesus and bind him and hand him over to the foreign tyrant for execution. Yet in both cases, as the scene in Gethsemane has made clear, it is God who wills these events. In the one case, Abraham's testing serves as the final act in a drama between God and Abraham in which Abraham's will is tested and he is prepared to be the father of a multitude of nations in accordance with God's promise to him (Genesis 17:4); he is to be the type of ethical monotheism, of radical obedience to the will of God. Abraham becomes the type of all faithful Jews, and indeed, beyond all ethnic boundaries, of any righteous person. In the other, Jesus, who has been proclaimed God's "beloved son" (Mark 1:11), is singled out as the instrument of God's will in the conflict with human wickedness. The sacrifice of Jesus is not so much the test of obedience (though it is that too) as the point of engagement

The German artist Gerhard Wilhelm von Reutern painted this dramatic image of the Akedah in 1849.

between the divine agent and the forces of destruction and death in the world. It is the point of transition from the world of death to the new age of life, which is anticipated in Jesus's resurrection.

Subsequent Christian retellings of the story of Jesus's Passion repeat this pattern of indirect allusion and variation. In John's Passion narrative Jesus "goes out, bearing his cross, to the place called the place of the skull" (19:17). This runs counter to the Synoptic story which has the soldiers

There are fourteen Stations of the Cross—traditional depictions of moments in Christ's Passion and death—including the six seen here, from the thirteenth-century Bamberg Cathedral. On the top row, from left to right, are stations six (Veronica wipes Christ's face), seven (Christ falls for the second time), and eight (Christ meets the women of Jerusalem). On the bottom row, from left to right, are stations nine (Christ falls a third time), ten (he is stripped of his garments), and eleven (he is nailed to the cross).

compelling Simon of Cyrene to carry the cross to Golgotha. Here, like Isaac, Jesus bears the means of his death with him on the way. This, intriguingly, is mirrored in rabbinic retellings of the Isaac story, which say that Isaac bears the wood like one who bears his cross. Later Christian exegesis picked up this motif and linked it to Christian experience of suffering. Christian willingness to bear suffering is seen as continuous with Abraham's faith: "Righteously also do we, possessing the same faith as Abraham, and taking up the cross as Isaac did the wood, follow Him." (Irenaeus, *Against Heresies*, IV.5.4). Later piety has elaborated this motif in the Stations of the Cross, which line the walls of Catholic churches and depict Jesus falling three times under the weight of the cross.

However, in Christian interpretation the Isaac story is not always directly related to Christ's death. Rembrandt in his etching (see page 95) has the angel not merely calling out to Abraham but actively restraining him by putting his arms around him. The story has become a depiction of divine protection, symbolized by the tender care of the guardian angel—a far step from the medieval rabbis who read this through their experiences of persecution and genocide.

By contrast the Danish philosopher Kierkegaard again celebrates in Abraham the man of faith. He calls Abraham's willingness to sacrifice his son the "teleological suspension of the ethical." In religious faith normal ethical laws and rules are suspended, as men and women embrace overriding goals or ends. The true "knight of faith" is one who moves beyond the world of ethics and enters a world which is governed by divinely given commands and promises. Abraham's greatness lies in his continued trust and faith in God against all the odds: it was not just a faith in the afterlife, in some final resolution of things, but in the here and now, a belief that God's promises would be made good, even after the apparent impossibility of Sarah's conceiving a child, in the face of God's command to sacrifice him. Kierkegaard's writings are part of a profound and personally costly protest against a bourgeois normalization of Christianity. His suspension of "normal" ethical standards remains dangerous and disturbing and brings out something of the strangeness and provocative nature of the original story, with its witness to a prodigious faith. If Abraham had not had faith, says Kierkegaard, he might heroically have sacrificed himself instead of Isaac. "He would have been admired in the world, and his name would never be forgotten; but it is one thing to be admired and another to become a guiding star that saves the anguished" (Kierkegaard, p. 21).

The Rich Afterlife of the Biblical Texts

The history of the reception of the biblical texts provides an almost inexhaustible fund of evidence of the vitality of these ancient writings. They have been read by very different faith communities in widely different circumstances and have generated readings of remarkable divergence as well as remarkable convergence. Explanations for this kind of fruitfulness are not easy to provide.

Part of the reason must lie in the diversity of contexts in which such texts are read; it is not surprising that the story of Isaac's binding will resonate differently with those under attack from marauding soldiers than with those who, say, have to face the rigors of life in a mountain village in Catholic Austria. There is also a major difference in the literary context of the Isaac story, as it is read by Jews and Christians. For Christians, with the massive concentration on the cross of Jesus in the New Testament writings, it is inevitable that

This etching, entitled _Abraham's Sacrifice_, was created by Rembrandt in 1655. The angel's arms encircle both Abraham and Isaac, and its wings fill the picture. Isaac is unbound and offers himself willingly; Abraham appears to be bemused, almost in despair.

the themes of the Akedah should be subsumed in their reading of the Passion. Isaac becomes the "type of the one who was to come" (Epistle of Barnabas 7.3) and the various motifs of the story are taken up and used, sometimes by way of contrast, in the narrative and discursive development of the Passion. For Jews there is more cause to reflect on the meaning of the story in the light of the history of Abraham's descendants.

But diversity of context will not explain all: there is in the texts themselves a richness and an ambiguity which invites diversity of interpretation. Images like Abraham's stretching out his hand, or his laying the wood on his son, strike profound chords in later writers and interpreters. The richness of imagery and metaphor in the biblical writings, in its narrative, poetry, and more discursive writing, is such that it is bound to lead to readings which draw freely on the experience of the readers. Here are stories and texts which widely diverse communities have been able to make their own, precisely because of their evocative nature. Nor are these closed, neatly tied up texts. They leave gaps and contain ambiguities which beg to be filled out and resolved. Some of the most fruitful texts, as we shall see, are those which are the most ambiguous.

The canonical status of the texts must account not only for the diversity and richness of the readings, but also for the way in which the narratives and discourses have themselves been reshaped. In the most striking example of this we saw how medieval retellings of the Akedah actually claim that the scriptural story relates Isaac's death. More often, it is a matter of emphasis, of selective reading: those elements in the biblical writings which resonate with a particular community over a particular period of time are the ones which will be stressed, to the exclusion or neglect of others. The results can be almost as dramatically different as the direct alteration of the Isaac story. But in either case what drives the process of interpretation is the same conviction: that these texts are normative for the experience of the community and that therefore the community's experience must somehow be reflected and represented in them.

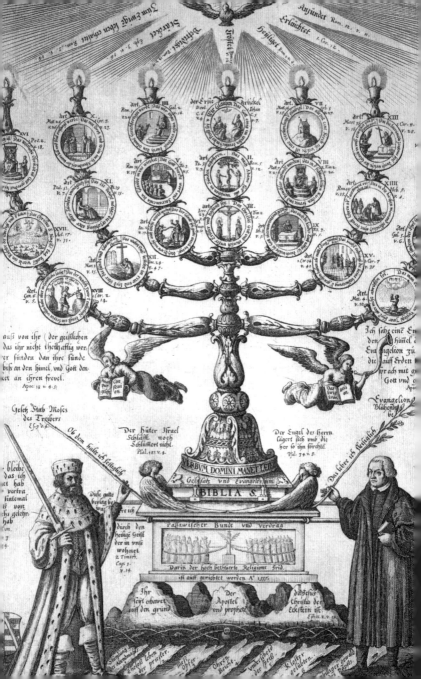

FIVE

The Bible and Its Critics

●

THIS CHAPTER WILL BE RATHER DIFFERENT from the previous one. Instead of looking in detail at the interpretation of one passage of scripture, I will focus on the most important developments in biblical criticism.

Criticism at root refers to the exercise of one's judgment. In effect, all interpreters of the Bible use their judgment to discriminate between possible meanings and senses of the text. They may well also want to give more weight to certain passages than others, to find meaningful interpretations for passages which seem to be of little obvious interest or whose apparent sense seems contradictory to expectation. This kind of intelligent, discriminating reading has been a perennial feature of Scriptural

The Augsburg Confession is a document containing twenty-eight articles of faith composed by a group of writers including Martin Luther and Philipp Melanchthon (see page 108) in 1530. It remains the most authoritative statement of Lutheran belief. This undated illustration of the Augsburg Confession's first twenty-one articles of faith, by Bohemian etcher Wenceslas Hollar (1607–77), depicts the Elector of Saxony, an ally of Luther's, on the left, with Luther himself on the right. The candlestick between them features twenty-one roundels illuminated with biblical scenes.

interpretation and is at the basis of present standard historical disciplines of text criticism, source criticism, and various forms of literary criticism, with which (almost) all biblical scholars work. However, the term "biblical criticism" can also have a much more antagonistic sense, when it is directed against dominant, ecclesiastical understandings of the Bible. Many of the developments which I will sketch out belong to this category. As will become clear, much of what is now standard critical practice was in fact pioneered by those who used it to attack orthodox readings.

First, such developments need to be set in their historical context. By the end of the Middle Ages, Christian interpretation of the Bible was more or less integrated with the official ideology of the church. The Bible contained stories about the creation of the world, the history of the Patriarchs, the election of Israel and the giving of the Law, the subsequent history of Israel in the Land, together with stories about Jesus and the early Christian missionary efforts and controversies. All this had been read in such a way as to give an integrated—and comprehensive—world history from the creation until the final judgment. The Bible, the church taught, told the story of God's response to Adam's sin: through the election of Israel and the giving of the Law, culminating in the sending of his son, the redemption of humanity through his crucifixion and resurrection, and the establishment of the church. In such a reading of the Bible, elements which play a central role in the Old Testament were played down: the giving of the Land, the Temple, the role of the Law and Israel in the salvation of the nations. Equally, motifs which are relatively minor were stressed, notably the notion of the Fall and of the universal corruption of the human race. The Old Testament was read as a precursor for the New, its main figures and their lives anticipating what was now fully realized in Jesus (as we saw with the comparison which the Fathers made between Isaac and Christ).

Thanks to the construction of this all-embracing narrative, the Bible became the source and measure of all knowledge: of cosmology, of history, of law, and of theology. In working such a story out, the theologians were, it is true, assisted by other disciplines. The Church Fathers of the first centuries drew freely on the Platonist philosophers; the medieval schoolmen, not without controversy, drew on Aristotle. But, officially at least, the Bible remained the final arbiter of truth. There was, seemingly, a remarkable fit between the Bible and the world in which medieval Christians lived. The Renaissance and the Reformation would, however, launch a two-pronged attack on this official consensus in the European West.

The Church under Attack: Challenges from Within

The Christian story just outlined was not the only version. There were deviant views within the church, which had itself split into East and West at the end of the previous millennium. Such divergent views were all the result of criticism of particular accounts of the Christian story. What is remarkable about such criticisms of the late medieval Christian story is that they attack its biblical basis. Luther's Reformation was the work of a professor of biblical studies. He used his formidable skills in reading ancient biblical texts, not only to make the Bible widely available in the vernacular, but also to challenge the accepted biblical worldview at a particularly sensitive point.

In one sense this was only a matter of minor changes to certain aspects of the overall picture, relating particularly to the role of the church in the salvation of individual souls. Late medieval doctrine taught that because God was a just judge, men and women, though redeemed by Christ's work, would still have to pay the penalty for their sins on earth; they could avoid or mitigate their justly deserved punishment, however, even after death, if they made use of the various penitential offices of the church. 2 Maccabees 12:43–45 offered scriptural support for prayers for the dead. The widespread acceptance of such doctrines bestowed enormous authority on the ecclesiastical hierarchy.

Luther challenged this perception of God's justice and forgiveness by scrutinizing its roots in scripture, notably in the Pauline epistles. The key text for him was in the Epistle to the Romans: "For in it the righteousness of God is revealed through faith for faith; as it is written, 'He who through faith is righteous shall live'" (Romans 1:17, quoting Habakkuk 2:4).

Martin Luther, the professor of biblical studies whose interpretation of Paul was the catalyst for the Protestant Reformation, is depicted in this portrait by Lucas Cranach the Elder (1472–1553). The inscription on the top of the painting—*In silentio et spe erit fortitudo vestra*—means "In silence and hope shall be your strength."

But what precisely did St. Paul mean, asked Luther, when he talked about the righteousness of God which was revealed by the Gospel? Did he refer, as the scholastics taught, to the righteous nature of God's handing out of justice, by which he condemns sinners and rewards the righteous? Or did he refer to the gift of righteousness which God conferred on unrighteous men and women? Either understanding could be supported by the Greek expression; what was decisive was the context in Romans, where Paul quotes a phrase from Habakkuk. It refers, Luther claims, to the gift of righteousness to those who believe, and who will in consequence have life (Dillenberger, p. 11).

This is a defining moment in the Reformation, and indeed in European history. For Luther the Bible now speaks about the liberation of men and women from the threat of God's law and punishment. It speaks about the grace and forgiveness of God given to all who hear the Gospel, and not just to those who submit to the penitential discipline of the church. In this way the Reformation sought to emancipate men and women from their bondage to the medieval church; they were now free to follow their vocations in the "worldly kingdom."

Thus this provocative new reading of the Pauline epistles provided the basis for a major transformation of the power structures and general ethos and attitudes of medieval Europe. What is interesting for our purposes here is how it was achieved. Luther argued against the dominant scholastic interpretation by appealing to the "grammatical sense" of scripture. That is to say, he used the standard methods of humanist philology and textual study to resolve what was an ambiguity within the Pauline text. In this way, reasoned, critical study of Paul was used to unseat the dominant, official understanding of the text.

Luther's critique of the dominant understanding of the Bible was applied from within the church. His preeminence within Protestantism would mean that such use of critical reason would become an essential (if not always exercised) characteristic of Protestant theology. In time, the range of critical methodologies would be expanded: historical, sociological, and literary criticisms would follow. Such exercise of critical reason would, of course, create yet more diversity of interpretation and the risk of still greater disunity. However powerful the orthodoxies which from time to time gripped Protestantism, the critical spirit would always be there, ready to subvert and loosen their hold.

The Church under Attack: Challenges from Without

Not all challenges to the received interpretation of the Bible came from within the church. The explosion of human knowledge and discovery which marked the end of the Middle Ages provided challenges of its own to a worldview which had been proclaimed to be all-encompassing and authoritative. In the first place, the discovery of new lands, broadcast in popular travelers' tales, showed up the geographical limitations of the biblical worldview. There were whole continents which had not even been dreamed of in the account of the world which had been spun out of the biblical narratives. Even if, by vigorous missionary activity, such lands could now be incorporated within Christendom, there remained a lasting question about the place which the new converts' forebears had had within God's universal plan of salvation.

Furthermore, the growth of historical sciences made it clear that the Bible's view of history was far from comprehensive. Historical research undermined the chronology of the Bible; it uncovered evidence of the existence of earlier civilizations not known to the biblical writers. The historical schema found in the Bible simply failed to encompass subsequent history. Daniel 7 speaks of four kingdoms and this, at the time of the Reformation, was widely adopted as a framework for world history. The four kingdoms were identified as those of the Chaldaeans, the Persians, Alexander the Great, and the Romans. The question was what had become of the Roman Empire? The German emperor claimed the title of Holy Roman Emperor, but where did that leave the French king—as his permanent vassal? It is not difficult to see the attractions to those who sought political security of the idea of a final (and therefore humanly unassailable) empire before the advent of Christ. But, like all attempts to stop the historical clock, it would hardly stand the test of time. Empires would come and go and the schema outlined in Daniel would simply not be complex or flexible enough to contain them.

If the view of history constructed out of the Bible was vulnerable to attack, then so too was its cosmology. Copernicus taught that the planets, including of course the earth, revolved around the sun. In the strange and bloodthirsty story in Joshua 10, Joshua, with the armies of the five kings of the Amorites at his mercy, prays to God, "Sun, stand thou still upon Gibeon; and thou, Moon, in the valley of Ajalon" (10:12). The prayer is answered: the sun and moon stand still for about a day, while Joshua's armies slaughter their opponents. The conflict between the cosmology in this story and Copernicus's understanding of planetary movements is clear. Even Luther and his disciple Melanchthon use the biblical story to dismiss the views of Copernicus. As Scholder points out, at this time, to all except those with considerable mathematical ability, Copernicus's theory of the revolution of the celestial bodies would have appeared as just one among a number of current speculations. Melanchthon, after citing a number of biblical passages, among them Joshua 10:12–13, categorically rejects Copernicus: "Strengthened by these divine testimonies, we hold fast to the truth and do not allow ourselves to be led astray from it by the blind works of

This 1816 painting by the English artist John Martin illustrates Joshua 10:12, in which the prophet commands the sun to stand still. This passage was cited by many in the sixteenth century as evidence against Copernicus's theory of planetary motion.

those who think it the glory of the intellect to confuse the free arts" (Scholder, p. 49, citing *Corpus Reformatorum* 13, cols. 216–17). However, the theologian Andreas Osiander, who prepared an edition of Copernicus's work published in Nuremberg in 1543, saw the seriousness of Copernicus's challenge more clearly and attempted to deflect it by arguing that Copernicus's views were mere hypotheses, useful for predicting the positions of the planets, but not intended to be factual statements about the workings of the universe. His calculations were, said Osiander, of great value but knowledge of the true causes of the movements of heavenly bodies is beyond the reach of our minds (Scholder, pp. 47–48).

Later debates between Darwinists and Creationists in the nineteenth century continued the same theme: Darwin's view of the origin of humankind in a line of mammals running through the apes

Martin Luther's collaborator
Philipp Melanchthon (1497–1560), coauthor of the Augsburg Confession (see page 98), is depicted in this 1532 portrait by Lucas Cranach the Elder.

clearly provided a very different account of human origins to that in Genesis. Notwithstanding the diversity and internal contradictions of the two accounts in Genesis 1 and 2, many Christians held that the Genesis account of direct divine intervention to create human beings should be treated as authoritative. Others came to see the Genesis stories as creation myths, not unrelated to other myths of this kind which circulated in the world of the Ancient Near East. This of course raised important questions about the relation of such myths to the scientific worldview.

The Enlightenment and the Rise of Historical Criticism

The internal church divisions of the Reformation period eventually led to religious wars which ravaged Europe from 1618 to 1648. This in turn led to a fierce reaction against all forms of religion and a search for emancipation from its authority, which is broadly referred to as the Enlightenment. The same period saw the rise of the empirical sciences and of certain kinds of rationalist and empiricist philosophy, all of which sought to base human knowledge and the conduct of human affairs on the unaided efforts of human reason. Such philosophies were powerful tools in the hands of those who sought political liberation in the absolutist states of Europe, whose authority rested on alliances with different churches. Human knowledge, said the French philosopher Descartes, should be based not on inherited beliefs and authority, but on "clear and distinct ideas," which could be discerned only by subjecting all our beliefs to radical scrutiny.

In England such tendencies found their particular manifestation in a loosely connected group of figures known as Deists. They sought to exclude religion from the management of human affairs. God, they said, was a distant figure who had created the world and then left it to its own devices, a watchmaker who had wound up the watch and then left it to run according to its own laws. They attacked the Bible, partly because it contained stories of divine interference with the operation of the physical ("natural") laws of the universe; and partly because it sought to impose a supposedly divinely instituted system of laws which were contrary to natural morality. In consequence, they ridiculed the miracle stories of the Bible, and attacked the morality of its main protagonists. They also attacked the doctrines by which orthodox Christians defined the authority of the Bible as the supreme vehicle of divine revelation and as such incapable of error. They pointed to the existence of inconsistencies and contradictions within the Bible itself. A favorite target of such attempts were the Resurrection narratives, which were the subject of a lively literature. In its more colorful forms the apostles were imagined in a trial setting and subjected to cross-examination to see if their case could be demolished. The finest example of this genre is Thomas Sherlock's 1729 "Trial of the Witnesses" (Stephen, vol. 1, pp. 203–4).

Such literature was disseminated relatively freely in Britain in the eighteenth century and found its way to France and Germany: there, however, draconian censorship curbed its distribution. This provides the setting for one of the more dramatic events in the history of biblical criticism, the so-called "battle of the Fragments." The main protagonists on the rationalist side in this dispute were a German scholar and schoolmaster, Hermann Samuel Reimarus, and Gotthold Ephraim Lessing, a playwright, literary critic, and philosopher-theologian. After a period in charge of the theatre in Hamburg where he wrote and put on the first truly German plays, Lessing took up a post as librarian to the Duke of Brunswick at Wolfenbüttel. Among his responsibilities was to prepare editions of the unpublished manuscripts in the library. While in Hamburg Lessing had become friendly with Reimarus and his family. Reimarus gave Lessing a manuscript which took up and developed Deist criticisms of the Bible, which he had not published for fear of imprisonment and public ostracism. Lessing decided to publish a series of fragments from the manuscript, pretending that it was something by an "unknown author" which he had found in the Duke's library. The first two published installments of the manuscript contained material which was drawn from Deist criticisms, though worked out with great thoroughness. Reimarus attacked the account of the miracle of the crossing of the Red Sea. He calculated painstakingly how long it would have taken to get the three million Israelites and all their baggage trains across the sea and concluded that the miracle would have consisted not so much in parting the waters as in getting the Israelites across before they were caught by the Egyptians. It was, however, the section on the contradictions contained in the Resurrection accounts which caused most offense and initiated a major public debate. Then in 1778 Lessing published a further Fragment entitled "Of the Purpose of Jesus and his Disciples."

In the first two paragraphs Jesus is portrayed as the preacher of a purified natural religion and an account is offered of his relationship to his contemporary Jews, which is something of a caricature. Like the Pharisees, says Reimarus, Jesus taught the doctrine of immortality. Unlike them he taught a righteousness purged of outward observance and free of hypocrisy. But then quite suddenly Reimarus introduces a question of a completely different kind: "Just as then there can be no doubt that Jesus

Hermann Samuel Reimarus Hermann Samuel Reimarus (1694–1768), above left, was the author of a book of rationalist biblical criticism that challenged the literal truth of the miraculous events described in the Bible, including the crossing of the Red Sea and Jesus's resurrection. It was also seen by many as initiating the quest for the historical Jesus. The German literary critic and playwright Gotthold Ephraim Lessing (1729–81), above right, published selections of Reimarus's book without divulging the name of its author.

pointed men in his teaching to the true great purpose of religion, namely eternal blessedness, so then it remains only to ask what purpose Jesus had for himself in his teaching and actions." The question is slipped in almost as an afterthought, as if we are here present at the moment when the question formed itself in Reimarus's mind. It is then followed by a remarkable passage where Reimarus lists, in rapid succession, the literary and historical problems which follow from such a question.

It is an odd question. It contrasts the "true great purpose of religion"— teaching a purified understanding of God and morality—with Jesus's "purpose for himself." As the sequel makes clear, what Reimarus is asking about is Jesus's engagement with the pressing concerns of his day: about Jewish aspirations for independence from Roman rule, about political power and its control and distribution. This was revolutionary. Earlier views of Jesus had portrayed him as a heavenly figure who had come to reveal heavenly mysteries and to institute a new religion. Such a revealed religion, which was beyond the reach of human reason, could sit easily with the authoritarian politics of the day. The questions which Reimarus posed about Jesus's involvement in the hopes, fears, and aspirations of people in the first century put Jesus back into the sphere of human history and politics. Such questions endangered the neat separation of the spheres of influence of church and state, where the church was responsible for men and women's supernatural goals and for the rest gave unquestioned support to the secular rulers. Could it be, as Reimarus suggested, that when Jesus announced the coming Kingdom of God, he was referring to the political overthrow of the ruling power, the Romans? In view of such disturbing political overtones in the published Fragments, it is hardly surprising that the Imperial Censor prohibited Lessing from making any further contribution to what had become a major public debate.

The questions which Reimarus raised were, in the first place, historical questions. To answer them one would have to employ all the tools available to the historian. Reimarus had already, in a remarkable way, spelled out some of the main tasks which such an inquiry into the life and thought of Jesus would involve. One would need to scrutinize the main sources for his life, the Synoptic Gospels, to see to what extent they had been subject to later revision and distortion. One would have to pay close attention to the contemporary sense of words and phrases. Jesus told his contemporaries to expect the coming of the "kingdom of God." But what did such a claim mean to Jesus's hearers?

The publication of Reimarus's work inaugurated a remarkably fruitful period of study, which Albert Schweitzer documented at the

Albert Schweitzer (1875–1965) had a distinguished career as a theologian, organist, and musicologist before training as a physician and spending the rest of his life as a missionary doctor in West Africa. He was the author of *The Quest for the Historical Jesus* (1906), a seminal book of biblical criticism, and was the recipient of the 1952 Nobel Peace Prize.

beginning of the twentieth century in his classic work *The Quest for the Historical Jesus.* What becomes clear in the course of this inquiry is the central importance of trying to place Jesus firmly in the context of first-century religious beliefs and movements. In practice the effort required for such a historical investigation was, and still is, enormous. One has only to think of the work that has been undertaken since 1948 in deciphering, translating, and editing the Dead Sea Scrolls to realize how much work is involved in preparing scholarly editions of the large number of relevant texts, even before the task of interpreting them and placing Jesus in relation to them can begin. The complexity of the task is further increased by the geographical spread of the sources and influences involved. On the one hand, the texts of the Old Testament have their roots in the wider world of the Ancient Near East; on the other, Christianity rapidly expanded into the Greco-Roman world of the Mediterranean outside Roman Palestine. To understand fully the place of the Bible in the history of the development of religious belief and practice in the ancient world one needs a truly formidable knowledge. Such an undertaking can only be a communal one.

I can give only a few examples. During the course of the nineteenth century a number of texts came to light which are now generally referred to as examples of "apocalyptic" thought. Previously, biblical examples of the genre had been available in Daniel and Revelation, but now a much wider range of such documents became known. Such documents purport, on the basis of some heavenly revelation, to reveal the mysteries of God's purposes, how the present "evil age" will be replaced by "the age to come" through God's dramatic intervention. A new heaven and a new earth will dawn. Could such texts throw light on what Jesus meant when he announced the coming of the "kingdom of God"? One such text attracted particular interest—the Testament of Moses. In it there is a description of the overthrow of the "kingdom of Satan" and its replacement by the "kingdom of God." Satan's rule would be done away with in a series of cosmic disasters and upheavals; the wicked would be punished and the righteous would enjoy eternal bliss. Such a text does indeed find echoes in the Gospels. In the stories of Jesus's temptation in the wilderness, Satan offers Jesus all the kingdoms of this world, which certainly implies that, for the time at least, they are his to offer. Similarly, in the so-called "Little Apocalypse" of Mark 13, Jesus prophesies just the sort of cosmic upheavals that one finds in the Testament of Moses.

What is one to make of texts like these? Some scholars, such as Johannes Weiss (in *Jesus's Preaching of the Kingdom of God*, 1892) and Albert Schweitzer, thought that they gave the closest approximation to Jesus's thought. Jesus expected a mighty act of divine intervention in history which would put an end to this evil age and would establish God's rule on earth. In this respect (if not in others) Jesus was of course mistaken. Others, disturbed by this conclusion, held that passages such as Mark 13 were later creations of the church; others that they were based on specific prophecies about the destruction of Jerusalem. In either case it was then possible to argue that the sense that Jesus attached to the phrase "the kingdom of God" was rather different to that found in apocalyptic literature. Some saw it as closer to the rabbinic notion of acceptance by the individual of God's will; others as referring to the divine intervention in history which was particularly associated with Jesus's own healing and preaching ministry; some have even wanted to place Jesus closer to first-century liberationist groups who sought to establish God's rule and Israel's independence by military means (though such views have met with little support among New Testament scholars).

What such discussions bring home is the extent to which the biblical texts and the figures who feature in them belong to a particular age and culture often very different, and indeed alien, to our own. Albert Schweitzer famously described this sense of the strangeness of the Jesus uncovered by the historical quest:

> The study of the Life of Jesus has had a curious history. It set out in quest of the historical Jesus, believing that when it had found Him it could bring Him straight into our time as a Teacher and Savior. It loosed the bands by which He had been riveted for centuries to the stony rocks of ecclesiastical doctrine, and rejoiced to see life and movement coming into the figure once more, and the historical Jesus advancing, as it seemed, to meet it. But He does not stay; He passes by our time and returns to His own.
>
> *Schweitzer, p. 397*

Criticism and Creative Readings

We have been looking at the ways in which critics both within and without the church sought to prise the Bible away from the authorized interpretations which it had received from the churches over a period of 1500 years. If church interpretations had succeeded in bringing the text and the experience of believers into a creative and apparently harmonious relation, the main thrust of such criticisms came from those who wanted to assert that their experience could no longer be accommodated within the church's biblical story. History, geography, and theories of evolution all burst the bounds of such interpretation. But if the Bible is prised away from its received interpretations, this does not mean that it ceases to be a source of social and cultural creativity. On the contrary, such fierce criticism of received interpretations can prepare the way for new and creative readings of the Bible. In their different ways, both Luther and those who engaged in the quest for the historical Jesus were seeking to make the Bible their own. Luther dramatically succeeded and thereby inaugurated a new family of Protestant readings. The work of the historical critics in attempting to reconstruct the life and teaching of Jesus—surely one of the most sustained intellectual undertakings in the world of the arts— has in turn generated a great diversity of readings of the Gospels. This process of historical quest and reconstruction ends with a much greater sense of the culturally conditioned nature of both the text and any subsequent interpretation. This has a twofold effect. On the one hand it issues a challenge to all attempts to equate the meaning of the Bible with any given interpretation. On the other, an awareness that the biblical texts themselves are the result of a creative dialogue between ancient traditions and different communities through the ages may have positive results. It may be a spur to further attempts to read the Bible creatively and imaginatively in contemporary contexts.

SIX

The Bible in the Postcolonial World

•

THE AREAS OF GREATEST GROWTH today for Christianity are in Africa and Asia, in countries which are emerging from a prolonged period of colonial domination, but which are still dominated in other ways by the economically more powerful nations in the world and their transnational institutions. Here the Bible is playing a remarkable role in the growth of new churches and new forms of church life. It has been drawn upon in the course of struggles for liberation from oppressive regimes, but it has also been the inspiration for those who have sought to develop forms of Christianity closer to their own traditional cultures. As the Bible has been translated into the vernacular, so new forms of belief and practice have grown up alongside the mainstream mission churches.

Charismatic and Pentecostal forms of Christianity, which base themselves on biblical accounts of spirit-filled activity in the early church, have grown with remarkable rapidity throughout the nations of Africa and Asia. This 2005 photograph shows a member of the Celestial Church of Christ in Cotonou, Benin, reading a prayer as she undergoes the ceremony of baptism.

In the early morning hours of October 12, 1492, the Italian explorer Christopher Columbus first landed on the shores of the "New World"—an island he named San Salvador, now part of the Bahamas. Columbus, like many colonizers of the era, believed his mission was divinely inspired. The American printmaking firm Currier & Ives created this depiction of Columbus's landing in 1892.

In all this the uses to which the Bible is being put are by no means uncontested: far from it. The Bible already had a history of use by colonizers and missionaries, which was in many cases far from liberating or respectful of local culture. This chapter will attempt to illustrate some of these very different readings and to identify the different sociocultural phenomena which have contributed to their development.

The Bible in Latin America

The history of the colonization of Latin America is one of the darkest episodes in European history. In the course of the first hundred years after Columbus's arrival, millions of people died through war, disease, and ill-treatment. In some areas the population was reduced by 80%. The Spaniards and Portuguese who colonized Central and South America were "given" the land by the Pope and encouraged to convert its population. Columbus, who "discovered" what is now the Bahamas in 1492, believed that his mission was part of the dawning of a new age, when the whole world would be united in Christ under the Pope to enjoy the final millennium before the Last Judgment. He was fond of quoting Isaiah 65:17: "For I am about to create new heavens and a new earth" and its echo in Revelation 21:1. The new age would embrace the whole earth; Mount Zion would be regained for Christianity and all would acknowledge the one true faith.

Moreover, by papal decree, the monarchs of Spain and Portugal were commanded to wage a holy war to support this missionary endeavor. Here the narratives of the conquest of Canaan in Joshua and Judges provided support not only for conquest, but also for the merciless killing of those who refused to submit. As one contemporary commentator on the widespread deaths, Fray Toribio, put it,

> Whether or not the great sins and idolatries that took place in this land cause it [the dying], I do not know; nevertheless I see that those seven idolatrous generations that possessed the promised land were destroyed by Joshua and then the children of Israel populated it.
>
> *Quoted in Prior, p. 61*

It is then not surprising that there have been those who have seen the Bible wholly as an instrument of oppression. When Pope John Paul II visited Peru, he received an open letter from various indigenous groups, inviting him to take back the Bible to Europe. Nevertheless, it was in Latin America that a powerful movement arose to rescue the Bible from its misuse in the colonial context.

Even at the time of the conquistadores there were voices which opposed the appalling treatment of the Indians and appealed very

John Paul II, we Andean and American Indians, have decided to take advantage of your visit to return to you your Bible, since in five centuries it has not given us love, peace, or justice.

Please take back your Bible and give it back to our oppressors, because they need its moral teachings more than we do. Ever since the arrival of Christopher Columbus a culture, a language, religion, and values which belong to Europe have been imposed on Latin America by force.

The Bible came to us as part of the imposed colonial transformation. It was the ideological weapon of this colonialist assault. The Spanish sword which attacked and murdered the bodies of Indians by day and night became the cross which attacked the Indian soul.

Richard, 1990a

differently to the Bible. Of course, the Bible was not needed to show that the treatment of the Indians was unjust and cruel beyond compare, but it could be appealed to as an authority in support of opposition to the oppressive treatment of the indigenous peoples. Bartolomé de Las Casas, the first priest ordained in the New World, a chaplain to the Spanish armies which conquered Cuba (1513), and a onetime slave owner, became a resolute opponent of the Spanish conquest. In this he was greatly strengthened by his reading of Sirach 34:21–26, which starts: "The bread of the needy is the life of the poor; whoever deprives them of it, is a man of blood. To take away a neighbor's living is to murder him; to deprive an employee of his wages is to shed blood." In his sermon at Pentecost in 1514 (Salinas, pp. 102–3), he asserted that an offering made to God without the practice of justice was stained with the blood of the poor: "Like one who kills a son before his father's eyes is the man who offers a sacrifice from the property of the poor." He was eventually ordered to withdraw to a monastery, attacked by his enemies as a heretic, and had his confessional withdrawn by the Emperor Charles V. After his death, Philip II of Spain approved measures to confiscate his works (Prior, p. 60).

This same emphasis on viewing reality from the perspective of the poor is found in the work of contemporary Latin American liberation theologians. It finds expression in their claims that God is on the side of the poor and that the church must therefore espouse a "preferential option for the poor"; and in the belief that the spiritual resources of the poor will provide a vital source of renewal for the church.

In *A Theology of Liberation* (1971), the Peruvian Indian priest Gustavo Gutierrez takes stock of nearly five hundred years of colonization and Western dominance. The end result is that the vast mass of the population live in great poverty and that the indigenous population are largely confined to the rural areas or the margins of the big cities. But for Gutierrez the Bible speaks of liberation—"For freedom Christ has set us free" (Galatians 5:1)—and such freedom must embrace political and economic freedom. Even though history teaches us how difficult it is to achieve such freedom, St. Paul still insists that the Easter experience of crucifixion and resurrection lies at the heart of "Christian existence and of all human life." In his preaching he reminds us of "the passage from the old man to the new, from sin to grace, from slavery to freedom." But when St. Paul talks about freedom, he is referring to "liberation from sin insofar as it represents a selfish turning in upon oneself . . . [B]ehind an unjust structure there is a personal or collective will responsible—a willingness to reject God and neighbor. It suggests, likewise, that a social transformation, no matter how radical it may be, does not automatically achieve the suppression of all evils" (Gutierrez, p. 35).

Liberation theology, that is to say, is an attempt to enlarge theology to take into account the social and political dimensions of human existence and so to reflect on the nature of the transformation required to bring about a just and peaceful world. Such transformation must by definition be social, a transformation of the structures and forms of society. But it cannot stop there: if it is to bring lasting peace and justice it requires an individual and collective change of heart.

This shift of theology from the sphere of private, individual salvation to the public and the social is the characteristic mark of liberation theology. It is grounded in a consideration of the nature of God as revealed in the narratives of the Bible, notably in the narratives of the Exodus, the Passion, and the Resurrection. Exodus speaks of God's response to the cries of his people in Egypt, suffering under slavery; the narrative of

Gustavo Gutierrez (1928–), a founder of Liberation Theology, said in a 1984 interview that the church in Latin America "has chosen to work for the poor and cannot turn back now." Father Gutierrez, who appears in this 1984 photograph, received the French Legion of Honor in 1993.

the death and resurrection of Jesus speaks of a hope for the transformation of the whole of human existence.

The choice of the Exodus narrative, of Israel's liberation from slavery in Egypt and subsequent entry into a "land flowing with milk and honey," is of course an obvious one: it speaks of a God who "takes the part of the oppressed." This means that "God's impartiality makes God love the orphan and the widow with preference. Curiously, but nevertheless logically, not making exception of persons means making a preferential option in a situation of oppression" (Pixley, p. 232, with reference to Deuteronomy 10:16–18). But if the choice of Exodus is an obvious one, it is also problematic, not least in the postcolonial situation of Latin America. For these narratives are closely linked with the narratives of the conquest of Canaan, which provided the ideological material for the colonial exploitation of Latin America, and indeed of other parts of the world. Some principle of selection is required if the narrative of liberation is not to end up as a narrative of conquest and genocide.

Pixley and Gutierrez take different routes. Pixley, following the United States theologian Norman Gottwald, offers a reconstructed history of Israel. This reconstructed history supplements and clarifies, rather than strictly contradicting, what is indicated in the Bible. In Gottwald's view, Israel developed out of a conglomerate of tribes in the "least populated" mountain areas of Palestine, who had migrated internally, fleeing the oppressive and warring kingdoms in the coastal plains. These were subsequently joined by the Hebrews who had escaped from Egyptian domination and these different groups eventually linked together in their belief in Yahweh, the God of the Hebrews. The narratives of the conquest and the destruction of the Canaanites are dismissed as later constructions. At the theological core of the narrative is the belief in the liberator,

Yahweh. "The fact that they succeeded in escaping enforced serfdom despite the powerful Egyptian army showed that God, who took the side of the poor in Egypt, was the true God" (Pixley, p. 236).

Gutierrez stays closer to the biblical text, but does so selectively. In his biblical meditation, *The God of Life*, there is no reference at all to the book of Joshua. What he does is to juxtapose the Exodus narrative with the preaching of Jesus and in particular his reading of Isaiah at his initial sermon in Luke's Gospel (4:18):

> The Spirit of the Lord is upon me,
> because he has anointed me to preach good news to the poor.
> He has sent me to proclaim release to the captives
> and recovering of sight to the blind,
> to set at liberty those who are oppressed.

Read through this lens, the narratives of the conquest of the land simply disappear; or, to put it another way, Jesus's sermon, with its weighting of the Old Testament traditions, itself provides a (canonical) principle of selection for the reading of the whole Bible. This of course contrasts with Gottwald's attempt to use historical reconstruction to correct/sanitize the biblical narratives.

The Bible in Africa

Colonialism in Africa extends into the very recent past. Most countries gained their independence only after the Second World War; some colonies were established as late as the second half of the nineteenth century. In Africa too the Bible could be used both as an instrument of oppression and of liberation. In South Africa, which was colonized by the Dutch in the seventeenth century and then annexed by the British at the beginning of the nineteenth, the stories of the Exodus and the entry to the Promised Land played a significant part in the emerging ideology of Afrikanerdom. As the British took over the running of the Cape and enforced their own legislation and taxation, Afrikaners began to leave and to set up new republics in Natal, the Orange Free State, and the Transvaal. It was easy to see such movements in terms taken from the Old Testament: the Afrikaners were fleeing from the British yoke, heading to the Promised Land which God had given to them. The fact that one of their grievances was that the British refused to let them continue to keep slaves did not stop them from drawing such parallels. But there again, slavery as an institution is not condemned in the Old Testament. There are—relatively—enlightened laws in the Pentateuch which seek to regulate but not to abolish it.

The Great Trek is the name given to the 1835–43 mass migration of the Boer people from the Cape Colony to the interior of what is now modern South Africa in an effort to escape British rule. This 1837 American engraving depicts the Voortrekkers on their journey.

Later Afrikaner ideology saw the Great Trek as a pilgrimage from bondage of a people "peculiar to God," pursued by the British army, into the land of promise, beset on all sides by unbelieving black "Canaanites." Thus a racist element is introduced into the appropriation of the texts. The identification of the black population with the Canaanites, in contrast to the white Afrikaners as God's peculiar people, sets a permanent barrier between the two peoples, as it was of course intended to do.

This mythology was buttressed by national acts of remembrance, centering on the vow which was said to have been made by the Afrikaners before the battle of Blood River. It was actively disseminated by the Broederbond, a Protestant organization formed in 1918 to promote Afrikanerdom. Here again biblical traditions are reread in the light of events in a community's history, and in the process that history is transformed.

Such readings of the Bible were not, however, allowed to go unchallenged. While much of the opposition to apartheid was based on secular or humanist ideologies, there is no denying the support which some leading figures within the churches gave to the struggle. It was common at the time to speak of the church as "a site of struggle" and this acknowledged the sense in which the church, its leadership, and its central symbols were contested. Nevertheless, church leaders like Desmond Tutu could indeed address the Afrikaner leaders on a particularly sensitive point: their use of the biblical traditions.

In this respect the collection of Tutu's writings, *Hope and Suffering*, is instructive. Tutu contests apartheid land policy, specifically the policy of clearing blacks from their traditional lands and relocating them in the so-called homelands. While Afrikaner ideology saw the black population as "Canaanites" cast out of their land because of their lawlessness, Tutu portrayed the black inhabitants of Duncan Village, who were under

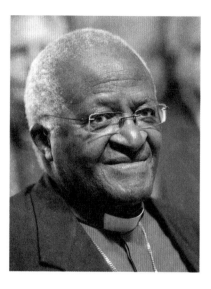

Archbishop Desmond Tutu (1931–), seen in this 2009 photograph, received the Nobel Peace Prize in 1984.

threat of forced removal, in terms of the narrative of Naboth's vineyard. In the story in 1 Kings 21 the king of Samaria offers to buy or to exchange the vineyard of one of his subjects, Naboth. Naboth refuses, because it is "the inheritance of his fathers." Jezebel, Ahab's foreign wife, intervenes and arranges to have Naboth falsely accused and stoned. When Ahab goes to take possession of the vineyard he is met by Elijah the prophet, who proclaims God's judgment on him in suitably colorful terms: "In the place where dogs licked up the blood of Naboth shall dogs lick your own blood" (21:19).

It is not difficult to see how Tutu can exploit this and draw the parallels between Naboth and the villagers, and between Ahab and Jezebel and the South African regime. The latter are the powerful who think they can treat the villagers as "unimportant people . . . You are nobodies in this country, this land of your birth." But "God cares about injustice, about oppression, about exploitation. . . . God cares that they want to move you from pillar to post." What the regime portrays as a matter of racial policy, of separate development, Tutu presents uncompromisingly as a matter of injustice, of disregard for the dignity of the blacks. "There is enough land for everybody in South Africa. It is just that some people are greedy and at the moment they are also powerful, and so they can satisfy their greed at the expense of others who they think to be unimportant and without power. But these are they whom God supports. South Africa, please remember the story of Naboth's vineyard" (Tutu, p. 42). Behind this lies the bloody history of the treatment of blacks under apartheid.

The story of Naboth's vineyard, 1 Kings 21, was used by Archbishop Desmond Tutu to challenge the Nationalist government's forced removals of black South Africans from their land. This educational biblical postcard from the 1950s depicts King Ahab confronting Naboth as he tends his vines.

The unspoken details of the Naboth story give Tutu's references to it an edge, almost an element of threat. It is not difficult to see why white South Africans reacted so powerfully against Tutu.

All of this is spoken from the point of view of black Africans who regard the land as their own, and this is, of course, contested by the Afrikaners. On this subject Tutu had already spoken powerfully in his open letter to John Vorster. There he writes to the then Prime Minister

> as one human person to another human person, gloriously created in the image of the self-same Son of God [Romans 8:29] who for all our sakes died on the cross and rose triumphant from the dead . . . sanctified by the self-same Spirit who works inwardly in all of us to change our hearts of stone into hearts of flesh [Ezekiel 36:26; 2 Corinthians 3:3] . . . as one Christian to another, for through our common baptism we have been made members of and are united in the Body of our dear Lord and Savior, Jesus Christ [1 Corinthians 12:13]. This Jesus Christ, whatever we may have done, has broken down all that separates us irrelevantly—such as race, sex, culture, status, etc. [Ephesians 2:14; Galatians 3:28]. In this Jesus Christ we are for ever bound together as one redeemed humanity, Black and White together.
>
> *Tutu, p. 29*

The language is shot through with biblical echoes and allusions; it creates a canonical framework within which to read the Bible. Rather than picking one leading theme, be it Exodus or possession of the Land, Tutu draws widely on themes from the Old and the New Testaments to provide a pattern of shared, basic beliefs within which to conduct the struggle for the tradition and the struggle for the interpretation of the history in which black and white are caught up together, like it or not. The racism of the Afrikaner readings of the conquest narratives is replaced with a Christian universalism, where social divisions are set aside in favor of a common humanity "in Christ."

Postindependence African readings

What happens when the colonial yoke is thrown off? How can the African churches, established and long run by Western missionaries, develop a theology and spirituality which is genuinely African in its expression and social embodiment? And what contribution can the Bible make to this undertaking? Clearly these are questions which extend beyond the scope of this book. Nevertheless the question of inculturation, of the rooting of Christianity in African culture, is one which has received specific attention within both the mainstream churches and those which have broken away, the African Independent Churches (AICs).

An interesting example of such postindependence readings is given by Musa Dube from Botswana. She recounts how AIC women in her country read the story of Jesus's encounter with a Canaanite woman, Matthew 15:21–28. The woman comes to Jesus asking him to heal her daughter, who is possessed. His disciples reject her and Jesus initially attempts to turn her away, claiming that he is "sent only to the lost sheep of the house of Israel," and saying: "It is not right to take the children's food and give it to dogs." However, the woman's reply—"Yes, Lord, but even the dogs eat of the crumbs which fall from their master's table"—is met with Jesus's praise of her faith and agreement to her request.

The African women's readings of this story were striking in a number of ways. In the first place the framework in which they read the story was strongly determined by the concept of Moya, Spirit. For them, the Spirit empowers people "to prophesy, heal the sick, assist those searching for jobs, restore family relations, ensure good harvest, good rains, and good reproduction of livestock, and to dispel the ever-intruding forces of evil from people's lives" (Dube, p. 112). So it is the Spirit, they said, which leads Jesus to the encounter with the woman; it is the work of the Spirit that Jesus should heal, teach, and preach. Moreover, the Spirit is for them inclusive. The AICs grew out of a rejection of "the discriminative leadership of missionary churches . . . Moya revealed to them the beauty of the gospel, its justice, and its inclusiveness over against the discriminative tendencies of the colonial church" (Dube, p. 124). Strikingly, one of the women explained the relation of Canaanites and Israelites as follows: "'Israelites were taken from Egypt, where they were enslaved . . . and sent to Canaan, a land flowing with milk and honey. This Canaanite woman with great faith illustrates for us what it means that their land flowed with milk and honey.'" As Dube comments: "This reading is a subversive postcolonial reading; it invalidates the imperial strategies that employ the rhetoric of poverty and lack of faith among the colonized to justify dominating other nations" (Dube, p. 125).

This inclusiveness, here related to Jesus's recognition of the Canaanite woman's faith, is shown in the readers' own willingness to borrow from traditions outside Christianity to make the story their own. The very concept of Moya is prevalent in African religions as the present activity of God, which "enters and empowers women and men." This taking up of a concept found in both religious traditions is "both a strategy of resistance and healing from imperial cultural forces of imposition, which depends on devaluing difference and imposing a few universal standards" (Dube, p. 125). At the same time the emphasis on the Spirit allows great freedom: members of the church can speak in the Spirit without other

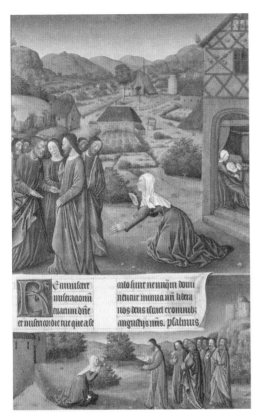

The story of Jesus and the Canaanite woman (Matthew 15:21–28) appears to portray Jesus rejecting a Gentile woman's request for help for her daughter because of her race. This page from *Les Très Riches Heures du duc de Berry*, an illuminated prayer book from the early fifteenth century, depicts the Canaanite woman in supplication at Jesus's feet.

authorization, official or biblical, and this is profoundly liberating for women, who play an important part in the life of the AICs.

Finally Dube notes that the emphasis on healing is central to the AICs' understanding of their faith. Healing activities of many kinds form a central part of their church life and are open to all. They embrace all aspects of life: "unemployment, breakdown of relationships, bad harvests, lost cows, evil spirits, bodily illness, and misfortune. . . . Through their claim that God's Spirit empowers them to heal these social ills, AICs join hands with God in a constant struggle against institutional oppression. They offer the promise and the solution. This space of healing becomes their political discourse of confronting social ills, not as helpless beings who are neglected by God, but as those who are in control and capable of changing their social conditions" (Dube, pp. 126–27).

Here healing, a motif which is prominent in the presentation of Jesus in the Gospels, but which has been largely played down in Western interpretations influenced by the Enlightenment, has been given a central position in the AICs' reception of the narrative. Thus there is twofold resistance to the dominant patterns of interpretation which have been purveyed by the mainstream churches. On the one hand, there is resistance to colonialist readings which have marginalized or excluded the colonized: here the Bible is appealed to as liberative, as empowering the poor, as open rather

Members of AIC (African Independent Church) congregations have developed ways of reading the Bible that draw creatively on their own indigenous traditions. In this 2006 photograph, members of Ibandlalama Nazaretha (the congregation of the Nazarites), founded by Isaiah Shembe (1870–1935), ascend the holy Nhlangakazi Mountain north of Durban, South Africa, in an annual pilgrimage. Worshippers gather at the base of the mountain, then climb barefoot to the top, where they pray and worship. The church, which is concentrated mainly in KwaZulu-Natal, has a membership of about four million.

than exclusive, as giving authority to women. On the other, there is an assertion of an alternative cosmology: belief in God's action as Moya and the understanding of the church as a community able to administer his healing action to all are, as Dube suggests, ways of countering the cruel physical and economic conditions which members of the AICs experience. They provide a framework of interpretation, a set of basic beliefs, in terms of which quite new realizations of the biblical texts can be achieved.

Use and Abuse

The history of colonial and postcolonial readings of the Bible provides a powerfully instructive study of its uses and abuses. It shows clearly the immense plasticity and fruitfulness of the biblical texts. They are open to the most diverse readings: the same texts, depending on how they are read, can bring either life or death to the same people. This might be enough to lead some to abandon their use altogether. On the other hand, as Lessing pondered two hundred years ago, rejecting the texts altogether means running the danger of turning one's back on vital resources for living.

Discussions like these bring us face to face with an acute dilemma. Those who can take a distanced look at the history of the conquest of Latin America cannot but be repelled by the uses to which the Bible was put in giving moral and religious support to the appalling treatment which the conquistadores meted out to the indigenous people. Nor can we simply dismiss their readings of the Bible as entirely arbitrary: the stories of the massacres of the indigenous people of the land of Canaan in the Bible are equally repugnant. On the other hand, we have strong contemporary evidence that the Bible *can* be used to bring comfort, strength, and liberation to people living under oppression, just as elsewhere we shall see how it has enriched the culture of both Jews and Christians.

There is too much that we should lose, if we were to turn our backs on it, dangerous as it is.

But how to use it? In the first place, critically. We need to be aware both of the different voices in the Bible and of the different emphases which readers can put on it. We need to learn to discriminate between these different voices and readings and to exercise our own moral judgment. Secondly, we should read charitably. By this I mean that we need to allow the creative, liberative, and constructive voices in the Bible to shape our understanding of the text, rather in the manner in which Desmond Tutu was able to draw together such elements to form a kind of lens through which to view the Bible and also the situation of apartheid South Africa. That is to say, we should not allow our own moral judgment to be overwhelmed by the darker side of the Bible. However, a critical and attentive reading of the Bible can inform and sharpen our moral sense and provide a moral and religious vision which can transform individuals and communities.

SEVEN

The Bible in High and Popular Culture

•

THE BIBLE IS ONE OF THE MAIN SOURCES of European culture. This is almost certainly understated. It might be better to say that the Bible is the primary and major source of European culture. In its various translations, it has had a formative influence on the language, the literature, the art, the music of all the major European and North American cultures. It continues to influence popular culture in films, novels, and music. Its language, stories, metaphors, types, and figures provide a vast cultural resource which is drawn on in a bewildering

John Milton's 1629 poem "Hymn on the Morning of Christ's Nativity" is considered by some critics to be the poet's first major work. Between 1808 and 1815, the English artist and poet William Blake painted a series of watercolors illustrating the poem, including this one depicting the annunciation to the shepherds (lines 109–11): "At last surrounds their sight / A globe of circular light, / That with long beams the shame-fac'd Night array'd . . ."

John Milton's epic poem *Paradise Lost*—an interpretation of the biblical story of Adam and Eve, their temptation by Satan, and their expulsion from the Garden of Eden—was intended, according to Milton, to "justify the ways of God to men." This 1866 engraving by the French artist Gustave Doré, depicting Satan at rest after the first day's battle in heaven, illustrates Book VI, line 406: "Now Night her course began . . ."

variety of ways, both consciously and unconsciously. From elaborate retellings of the narratives in great novels like Thomas Mann's *Joseph and his Brothers* and Bach's musical representation in the *St. Matthew Passion*, through Rembrandt's intimate depictions of biblical scenes and narratives, to echoes of biblical metaphor and motifs in poetry and fiction, there is a huge range of use. Poets like Milton and Blake must remain unintelligible to those without a knowledge of their biblical sources; in other writers it is more as if they are drawing on some "great code" which is so much part of the cultural heritage that it is almost impossible to escape from it, whether one is conscious of its biblical origins or not.

· · · · ·

> The Bible is clearly a major element in our own imaginative tradition, whatever we may think we believe about it. It insistently raises the question: Why does this huge, sprawling book sit there inscrutably in the middle of our cultural heritage like the "great Boyg" or sphinx in Peer Gynt, frustrating all our efforts to walk around it?
>
> *Northrop Frye,* The Great Code: The Bible and Literature*, pp. xviii–xix*

· · · · ·

Biblical Retellings: The Bible in Music

The retelling of biblical narratives is a feature of the Bible itself. The stories of the books of Kings are repeated in the books of Chronicles; the Gospel story is retold three times. Moreover, as we have already seen, this tradition of retelling appears in Jewish and Christian writing from as early as the second century BCE. The story of Abraham's binding of Isaac is retold in the Book of Jubilees, in Josephus's

Antiquities, in Midrash, and in the poetry of the Middle Ages. Such retellings helped the hearers to make sense of their own experience; they also served to inscribe their experience in their canonical texts. Such reciprocity—the use of the cultural language of the Bible to make sense of new and often disturbing experience and the reshaping/rereading of the canonical texts in the light of such bewildering and anomalous experience—would encourage writers, artists, and musicians to continue this tradition outside the precise confines of the community of faith.

· · · · ·

IDIOMS OF BIBLICAL ORIGIN

Here are some common expressions in English which derive from literal translations of Hebrew idioms into English in the Authorized Version:

Job 19:20

My bone cleaveth to my skin and to my flesh, and I have escaped with the skin of my teeth. (In the Revised Standard Version this becomes "by the skin of my teeth.")

Isaiah 3:15

"What mean ye that ye beat my people to pieces, and grind the faces of the poor?" saith the Lord GOD of hosts.

Micah 7:17

They shall lick the dust like a serpent, like the crawling things of the earth; they shall come trembling out of their strongholds, they shall turn in dread to the LORD our God, and they shall fear because of thee.

Numbers 22:31

Then the LORD opened the eyes of Balaam, and he saw the angel of the LORD standing in the way, and his drawn sword in his hand; and he bowed down his head, and fell flat on his face.

· · · · ·

The development of such a process of retelling of the biblical narratives outside a specific church context must have been gradual. The medieval Passion Plays are a good example of the way in which the telling of the story spills out of the church confines onto a wider stage. The story of the Oberammergau Passion Play, which originated as a thanksgiving for deliverance from the plague, indicates how such popular reenactments of the Passion may have a very specific reference to events in the community's history. Such plays are expansions of the medieval liturgical practice of reading or chanting the Gospel Passion narratives in dramatized form—different voices representing the evangelist, the various

· · · · ·

The Bavarian village of Oberammergau was stricken by the plague in 1633. In gratitude for the end of the attack, the villagers vowed to perform a Passion Play every ten years. All the actors come from the village; there are 124 speaking parts and hundreds of villagers take part in the crowd scenes. The action starts with Christ's entry into Jerusalem and ends with the Resurrection. Each scene is introduced by a tableau representing a scene from the Old Testament which prefigures the action to come. The scene with Christ before Pilate is paired with Daniel's appearance before Darius.

· · · · ·

characters, and the crowd. This musical tradition was developed in the seventeenth century with the emergence of opera, oratorio, and cantata and their attendant forms of aria, recitative, and chorale. New texts for the arias and chorales were added to the text of the Gospel with the result that it was possible to give greater expression to the emotions of the participants. By the beginning of the eighteenth century this tendency had gone so far that Passions were written which no longer adhered to the text of the Gospels, but were a complete retelling. Bach's two surviving Passions, the *St. John Passion* and the *St. Matthew Passion*, still retained the medieval practice of presenting the full text of the Gospel, though in the *St. John Passion* he added passages from Matthew's Gospel (the evangelist's comment after the cockcrow and the earthquake after Jesus's

This scene from the 1900 Oberammergau Passion Play dramatizes Christ's resurrection, an event that is referred to quite variously in all four Gospels. According to Matthew 28:4, the sentries dispatched by Pontius Pilate to secure the tomb were astonished to see Christ rise from the dead: "And for fear of him the keepers did shake, and became as dead men."

death) to provide additional color. Overall the earlier *St. John Passion* is sparer, so that the text of the Gospel stands out more clearly. Even so, the music clearly underlines certain themes. In the first place, the crowd parts in the Gospel provide the opportunity for Bach to display his dramatic skills. The centerpiece of the crowd's contribution comes in the trial and crucifixion, where there is a formal symmetry between the various passages which the chorus sings (see below).

In Bach's setting 1 and 2 correspond to 7 and 8; the same music occurs in 3 and 6; 4 and 5 are musically identical and so form the center of this section. Between them Bach sets a chorale:

> Through your prison, Son of God,
> Freedom has come to us.
> Your dungeon is the throne of grace,
> The place of deliverance for all the faithful.
> If you had not taken slavery upon yourself,
> our slavery would be eternal.

· · · · ·

CROWD PARTS IN THE TRIAL AND CRUCIFIXION

1. "Not this man, but Barabbas."
2. "Hail, King of the Jews."
3. "Crucify him, crucify him."
4. "We have a law and by our law he ought to die, because he made himself the Son of God."
5. "If thou let this man go, thou are not Caesar's friend; whosoever maketh himself a king speaketh against Caesar."
6. "Away with him, away with him, crucify him!"

7. "We have no king but Caesar."
8. "Write not, The King of the Jews; but that he said, I am the King of the Jews."

· · · · ·

The effect of this is twofold: in the first place there can be no denying the way in which the opposition of the Jews and their part in Jesus's condemnation to death is emphasized. This is certainly an emphasis in the Gospel text, but the gusto with which the choir calls for his crucifixion underlines their participation dramatically, as does the musical structuring of these numbers. Nevertheless it is not the centerpiece: this is provided by the chorale. Here Lutheran notions of Christ's paying the penalty for human sin, of humanity as weighed down by the burden of its guilt, are central. The focus of the Passion is on the individual's struggle for peace and freedom from guilt. But the musical force of the presentation of the Jewish crowds remains and is intensified in the later *St. Matthew Passion*, which also develops the arias and chorales in the same Lutheran direction.

Bach's Passions were originally written for the Lutheran observance of Holy Week in Leipzig in the first part of the eighteenth century. They still remain a firm part of Lutheran observance (though now rarely given as part of a church service), but have also made their way effortlessly into the concert hall. This ability of liturgical works to transfer into a broadly secular context is, at least in part, an eloquent testimony to the way in which great liturgical compositions address and enable the participants to confront the *grandeurs et misères* of human existence.

A similar expansion of liturgical form occurs in Britten's *War Requiem*, where the composer sets the First World War poems of Wilfred

This photograph was taken on May 29, 1962, at a rehearsal inside the newly rebuilt Coventry Cathedral in Coventry, England, for the premiere of Benjamin Britten's *War Requiem*, which took place the following day. The British tenor Peter Pears (1910–86) sings at left; the German baritone Dietrich Fischer-Dieskau (1925–) listens at right. The work was commissioned for the reconsecration of the cathedral, which had been virtually destroyed by Luftwaffe bombs in 1940.

Owen alongside the text of the Requiem Mass. At the offertory, where the elements of bread and wine are presented for the sacrifice of the mass, the boys' choir prays for deliverance for the souls of the faithful from the pains of hell and that Michael might lead them into holy light "which, of old, Thou didst promise unto Abraham and his seed." This last phrase is taken up in an extended fugue which leads into Owen's reworking of the Akedah narrative:

> So Abram rose, and clave the wood, and went,
> And took the fire with him, and a knife.
> And as they sojourned both of them together,

Isaac the first-born spake and said, My Father,

Behold the preparations, fire and iron,

But where the lamb for this burnt-offering?

Then Abram bound the youth with belts and straps,

And builded parapets and trenches there,

And stretched forth the knife to slay his son.

When lo! an angel called him out of heav'n,

Saying, Lay not thy hand upon the lad,

Neither do anything to him. Behold,

A ram, caught in a thicket by its horns;

Offer the Ram of Pride instead of him.

But the old man would not so, but slew his son,—

And half the seed of Europe, one by one.

The British poet Wilfred Owen (1893–1918), whose poems form part of the text of Britten's *War Requiem*, was killed in the Battle of the Sambre during World War I, one week before the Armistice. In a preface to a volume of his poems, Owen wrote, "I am not concerned with Poetry. My subject is War, and the pity of War . . . All a poet can do today is warn." This photograph of Owen appeared in a 1920 edition of his poems.

As the soloists repeat the last line of the poem, the boys' chorus enters again with the words of the offertory and its reference to the promises to Abraham and his seed.

As in Rabbi Ephraim's poem (see pages 85–86), the story is broken under the weight of the poet's suffering. But the Rabbi's poem, even though Isaac dies, still ends with his resurrection and the vindication of Abraham's faith. Owen's "old man" slays the young of Europe "one by one" on the parapets of the trenches, refusing to accept the Ram of Pride for his sacrifice. In Britten's setting the voices of the soldiers are accompanied by the choirs pleading for the resurrection of the slain: "make them, O Lord, to pass from death unto life, which thou didst promise to Abraham and his seed." By comparison with the Rabbi's poem, there is here a far more violent rupture between the retelling and its original. The very ground of the story—Abraham's faith in God who will preserve him and his forebears—is questioned by the action of Abraham toward his own son. The son's question "My Father . . ." is repeated by the tenor and contrasts the son's innocent trust with the senseless slaughter that follows. There is no looking back to the inherited, archetypal faith of Abraham: only the image of the damaged wayside crucifix, of the crucified deserted by his followers but with the soldiers clustered around, offers any hope:

One ever hangs where shelled roads part.
In this war He too lost a limb,
But now His disciples hide apart;
And the soldiers bear with him.

Near Golgotha strolls many a priest,
And in their faces there is pride

That they were flesh-marked by the Beast
By whom the gentle Christ's denied.

The scribes on all the people shove
And bawl allegiance to the state,
But they who love the greater love
Lay down their life; they do not hate.

Owen's poem is interspersed with the Latin text of the Agnus Dei: O Lamb of God, Who takest away the sins of the world, grant them rest. The effect of his reworking of the Abraham story is to force a reevaluation of the tradition: to challenge the priests and scribes who have been corrupted by national pride and unquestioning obedience to the state. The slain lamb replaces the Ram of Pride.

Biblical Images in Art

Although the Bible consists solely of written material, it has spawned a whole world of imagery and pictorial art. Again, this initially starts within the worshiping communities of the Bible, more so among Christians than Jews, who were far more cautious about the use of images in their synagogues. Some of the earliest forms of such art were in church iconography, paintings, mosaics, frescos, and stained-glass windows which decorated and instructed at the same time: the Bible of the poor. The great Italian masters like Giotto in the Scrovegni chapel in Padua (ca. 1305) and Michelangelo in the Sistine Chapel (1508–13) worked to a grand scheme. Giotto's frescos run in four bands along facing walls of the chapel, depicting (from top to bottom) scenes from the life of Mary, scenes from the life of Christ, and allegorizations of virtues and vices.

Michelangelo's depiction of the Final Judgment adorns the altar wall of the Sistine Chapel in Rome. It was completed between 1535 and 1541—thirty years after the artist had completed the Sistine Chapel ceiling.

On the triumphal arch leading into the sanctuary there is a depiction of the Annunciation, on the west wall a portrayal of the Last Judgment. As in the Sistine Chapel, the pictures are not only there to remind the congregation of the individual stories from the Bible, but to present a comprehensive worldview, with its concentration on redemption through the incarnation, with its preparation in the life of the Virgin. The personal

This fresco of the Lamentation over the Dead Christ—the demonstrations of mourning that followed Christ's death, after his body was removed from the cross—was painted by the Florentine artist Giotto. It is one of a series of frescos that the artist executed for the walls of the Scrovegni Chapel in Padua, Italy, which was consecrated in 1305.

implications of such a view of the world are made plain in the panels depicting the vices and the virtues and in the stark contrasts of the Last Judgment. In later Renaissance art such schemes are expanded and scenes from the Old Testament are compared and contrasted typologically with those of the New.

For all the tenderness and humanity of Giotto's depiction of the New Testament characters, his work remains in a sense schematic, presenting the official doctrine of the church in a set format. The art of the Renaissance introduces a more individualistic, more personal element into its depiction of biblical scenes. Donatello's wonderful bronze of David (ca. 1446–60) is a study of boyish beauty and introspection, Masaccio's depiction of the expulsion of Adam and Eve from the Garden, in the Brancacci chapel in Florence (ca. 1425), is an extraordinary study of human desolation and loss. A century later Grünewald, in his Isernheim altar (ca. 1513–15), will spare no effort in portraying the physical torture and suffering of the crucified Jesus. Whereas in the other panels of the altar the angelic, heavenly world hovers in the background or actively intervenes, here all is dark, bereft of the divine glory: it is an extraordinary portrayal of the Son of God's identification with the godforsakenness of the afflicted.

There is a similarity of theme in the oil painting *The Entombment* by Rembrandt in the Hunterian Art Gallery in Glasgow, though it is a very different treatment. Here Christ's body is being laid in a tomb cut into the rock, with an entrance to the right. An old man holds his shoulders; the main weight of the shroud in which the body is being lowered is taken by a younger man, behind whom stands a figure supporting himself on the rock; on the right a turbaned, kneeling figure holds the shroud at his ankles. To the left of this group is a woman holding a torch and shielding it with her hand; next to her stands an old bearded man. Behind this main group, and to the right there is a further group of figures, dominated by a large figure carrying a lantern. A remarkable feature of the painting is its use of light and dark: one's eyes have to get used to the subtlety of the play of light, which only just allows the outlines of some of the figures on the right to emerge.

There is a similar Entombment in Munich, which Rembrandt painted between 1636 and 1639 and it is likely that the Glasgow painting was painted some time before this. The Munich work forms part of a set of paintings, which also includes an Adoration of the Shepherds. Strikingly, the Adoration of the Shepherds in Munich closely resembles the Glasgow Entombment, both in its composition, which is almost its mirror image, and in the way that the light seems to radiate from the infant Christ. Thus the figures in the Glasgow painting seem to be subtly caught between grief, tenderness, and adoration. Interestingly, Rembrandt overpainted the figure of a prostrate woman at Christ's feet with the present kneeling figure. It seems that he preferred a figure kneeling in adoration to that of one prostrate in grief.

The relation of Rembrandt's painting to the Gospel text is complex. Matthew's account of Jesus's death and burial, in particular, contrasts the dramatic events which accompanied his death—the rending of the Temple veil, an earthquake, with rocks split, tombs opening, and "saints appearing"—with the entombment and sealing of the tomb with a large rock (Matthew 27:51–54). He describes Joseph of Arimathea's request to Pilate for the body and Pilate's agreement to the request and continues:

> And Joseph took the body, and wrapped it in a clean linen shroud,
> and laid it in his own new tomb, which he had hewn in the rock;

Rembrandt painted this version of *The Entombment* around 1630. It now hangs in the Hunterian Art Gallery at Glasgow University.

and he rolled a great stone to the door of the tomb, and departed. Mary Magdalene and the other Mary were there, sitting opposite the sepulchre.

Matthew 27:59–61

In a number of paintings, engravings, and sketches one can see Rembrandt working on the details which the text omits: the manner in which the body was taken down from the cross and was carried

Rembrandt completed another version of *The Entombment* in 1639, a version that can be seen in the Alte Pinakothek museum in Munich, Germany. The painting, above, is part of a group that also includes *The Adoration of the Shepherds*, above right.

to the tomb, the scene inside the tomb. In the Munich painting, the eye is led away from the figures in the tomb. Through a hole in the rock the crosses can be seen. In the Glasgow painting, by contrast, the entrance is obscured: it is almost as if one were in the sealed

tomb. The sealing of the tomb is echoed in the closed-in feeling of
the painting. But equally Rembrandt allows the viewer to see what
it is that will roll back the stone: the power of the new life which
resides in the dead Christ, mourned, cherished, and adored by his
few remaining friends and family. Here Rembrandt is indeed an
interpreter of his text.

Biblical Symbolism: The Bible in Metaphor and Concept

It is not just in the retelling of the great stories of the Bible, whether in literature, music, pictorial art, or indeed film, that the Bible has shaped and informed the European cultural heritage. In *La Dolce Vita*, Fellini punctuated his account of the decadence of modern Roman society with images and motifs taken from the Book of Revelation. Ingmar Bergman's *The Seventh Seal* uses similar motifs in his dark film of the plague. The language, metaphors, and concepts of the Bible permeate our culture in endless kinds of ways: from the turn of phrase which may add a twist to a scene, through the exploitation of major biblical metaphors and concepts which may shape a work as a whole, however they are received or reworked (or indeed rejected), to works which reflect on the role of the Bible itself.

Lest it be thought that such influences are to be found only in works of past decades, let me take an example from a current writer, Margaret Atwood. In *The Handmaid's Tale* Atwood creates the world of Gilead, an authoritarian post-nuclear state in North America, where human fertility has dropped alarmingly, and where a class of "handmaids" has been created, who are allocated to childless couples among the leadership with the specific task of bearing children. They are tightly controlled and subject to fierce punishments and eventual banishment to the colonies or execution if they fail to conceive or if they rebel.

The biblical word "handmaid" is a convenient euphemism for their enslavement, having its root in the Hebrew *amah*, meaning maidservant or female slave. The key sense for the novel is given by the reference to the slave girl Bilhah (see Genesis 30:1–9), whom Rachel gives to Jacob, out of her jealousy for her sister Leah's success in child-bearing. This is what Offred, the narrator of the tale, refers to as "the moldy old Rachel and Leah stuff we had drummed into us at the Center" (Atwood, p. 99). It also resonates with the story of Abraham, Sarah, and Hagar. Hagar is the slave given to Abraham when Sarah fails to conceive, who is subsequently driven out into the desert with her son when Sarah succeeds (Genesis 21:8–21). Perhaps most significantly, it echoes Mary's words at the Annunciation, "Behold the handmaid of the Lord; be it unto me according to thy word" (Luke 1:38). In short, the term is connected with slavery, sexual exploitation, and submissiveness.

However, there is another more subversive strand of narrative which is linked to the use of the term "handmaid" in the Bible, which embraces figures like Abigail (1 Samuel 25), who averts the threat of the destruction of her people by running to David from her husband Nabal, a series of "wisewomen" who advise the Jewish kings, and finally Judith, who tricks the Assyrian general Holofernes when she offers to tell the Assyrians a secret way into the city of Bethulia. She brings her own provisions and refuses to eat what Holofernes offers, assuring him, however, with heavy irony: "As thy soul liveth, my lord, thine handmaid shall not spend those things that I have, before the Lord work by mine hand the things that he hath determined" (Judith 12:4). Finally she goes to his tent, eats and drinks with him, and when he is thoroughly drunk, cuts his head off with his own sword (13:4). The story is reminiscent of an earlier killing of a foreign invader, Sisera. Here Jael, the wife of Heber, takes the fleeing general into her tent and drives a tent peg through his temples (Judges 4:22).

This too finds its echoes in the tale. Offred, after she has kissed the Commander in his room (something strictly forbidden and

This depiction of the biblical heroine Judith holding the severed head of the Assyrian general Holofernes was painted by Andrea Mantegna around 1495.

compromising), contemplates removing the lever from the toilet cistern and then "driv[ing] the sharp end into him, suddenly, between his ribs. I think about the blood coming out of him, hot as soup, sexual, over my hands" (Atwood, p. 150). Thus the tale picks up age-old themes about the struggle of women against men's domination and overarches the present by setting them in a putative future world.

The book also comments directly on the role of the Bible in all this. The Commander reads the Bible, or rather the passages which are carefully selected and bookmarked, to the household.

> He crosses to the large, leather chair reserved for him, takes the key out of his pocket, fumbles with the ornate leather-covered box that stands on the table beside the chair. He inserts the key, opens the box, lifts out the Bible, an ordinary copy, with a black cover and gold-edged pages. The Bible is kept locked up, so the servants won't steal it. It is an incendiary device: who knows what we'd make of it, if we ever got our hands on it? We can be read from it, by him, but we cannot read. Our heads turn towards him, we are expectant, here comes our bedtime story. . . . the usual story, the usual stories. God to Adam, God to Noah. Be fruitful, and multiply, and replenish the earth. Then comes the moldy old Rachel and Leah stuff.
>
> *Atwood, pp. 97–99*

As David Jasper comments: the tale "plays upon the power of the Biblical canon and the way in which it has been protected by authority and used as an instrument of social control. Indeed, part of Atwood's purpose is to indicate the dangers of our *not* knowing this foundational book of our culture, which still permeates our customs and social order in manifold, hidden ways. The Republic of Gilead is perhaps not so futuristic but in a sense a nightmarish vision of our *own* society" (Jasper, pp. 47–48). The tale also points to the hidden subversive resources of the Bible, which needs to be kept under lock and key, "like an incendiary

The 1990 film *The Handmaid's Tale* was adapted from Margaret Atwood's 1985 novel of the same name. In this still from the film, the Commander, played by Robert Duvall, and Offred, played by Natasha Richardson, meet in a dangerous encounter.

device: who knows what we'd make of it, if we ever got our hands on it?" The experience of the "handmaids" would lead them to very different stories and put a very different complexion on the work as a whole.

The Root of Culture

This chapter has attempted to give a brief impression of the sheer fecundity of the Bible, of its ability to inspire an immense variety of cultural expressions, of the very different things that people can make of it, "once they get their hands on it." Part of the problem for our society lies in its widespread ignorance of the Bible. The handmaids in Atwood's tale know only what they are told and are unaware of its subversive capabilities.

To the extent that we are not even aware of those themes and motifs from the Bible which hold us and condition our social mores, our position may be even worse. If we do not know what it is that holds us, how can we criticize, let alone recover the biblical elements in our culture? The way to a deeper appreciation and critique of our cultural heritage is barred. So too is the way to a more liberating and redemptive use of the Bible.

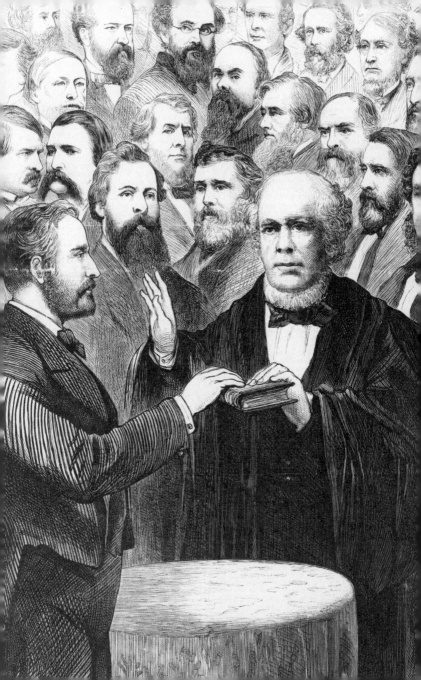

EIGHT

The Bible in Politics

•

THE NARRATIVES, LAWS, AND PROPHECIES of the Old Testament/Hebrew Bible make at least one thing clear beyond doubt: for the writers, God's will and instruction to his people embraced the whole of life. What the people did under leaders like Moses and Aaron, or under the later kings, was a matter to be judged by the Law of God. They owed their existence as a people to God; if they kept his Law he would protect and care for them; when they abandoned it, he would bring judgment, exile, and slavery on them. The New Testament carries a less clear message: its major figure, Jesus, advocates an ethic which to some has seemed unworldly or utopian: nonresistance to evil, love of enemies, refusal to swear oaths. Some of his sayings can be taken to make a sharp separation

The integral relationship between religion and politics is symbolically strengthened by the practice of resting one's hand on a Bible while taking an oath—a practice that some Christians renounce, based on Matthew 5:34. This 1873 engraving depicts President Ulysses S. Grant taking the oath of office, administered by Salmon P. Chase, chief justice of the Supreme Court.

between the religious and the worldly sphere: "Render to Caesar the things that are Caesar's and to God the things that are God's" (Matthew 22:21); "My kingdom is not of this world" (John 18:36). Paul encourages his Roman correspondents to obey the powers that be (Romans 13:1), but he himself falls foul of the civil authorities. In the Book of Revelation Rome is portrayed as the whore of Babylon and the seer looks to its destruction and the time when God's rule will extend over the whole world (Revelation 17:1–6). Sometimes, it seems, the New Testament sets

The story of Peter and the tax collector in Matthew 17:24–27 is sometimes cited as evidence of Jesus's belief that spiritual authority does not necessarily overrule secular or political authority. This painting by the Italian artist known as Masaccio, completed in the 1420s, depicts the events: Jesus instructs Peter to go to the sea and extract a coin from the mouth of the first fish that comes to the surface. Peter does this, then gives the coin to the tax collector on his and Jesus's behalf.

out the ethics for a world which will come into being only when the present rulers of the world have been swept aside and a new heaven and new earth established; at others it seems more concerned to allow the

I am puzzled about which Bible people are reading when they suggest religion and politics don't mix.

Desmond Tutu, Christian Aid poster

secular world to have its proper sphere of operation, while itself focusing on the affairs of the heavenly kingdom.

Given that the biblical texts contain such a complex and in part contradictory message, we may expect their use and impact itself to have been similarly diverse. We have already seen something of this. Colonial readings justified the conquest by Christians of lands in Latin America and Africa, the subjugation of indigenous people and even their extermination. On the other hand, the same Bible could also be a powerful instrument for the liberation of colonized peoples. In this chapter we shall look at some other areas of political life where the Bible has been influential in forming political doctrines and practice and look further into the complexity and diversity that this has produced.

The Bible and Political Authority

Heikki Räisänen, a Finnish scholar, once claimed that Romans 13:1 ("The powers that be are ordained of God") was the most influential single text in the Bible. This may well be true. Appeal to such a text can give a covering of theological respectability and authority to the most iniquitous and callous regime, and such appeals have therefore been common. One of the classic treatments of these themes is Luther's *Secular Authority: to what extent it should be obeyed*. Published in the early years of the Reformation (1523), it attempted to define the authority and duties of the princes. While it sets out the positive grounds for their authority, the tone is undeniably critical, stressing "what they [the princes] should omit and not do" (Dillenberger, p. 365).

Luther is in no doubt that the princes are indeed authorized by God to pursue their office and that such an office includes the pursuit and capital punishment of evil doers. "We must firmly establish secular law and the sword, that no one may doubt that it is in the world by God's will and ordinance" (Dillenberger, p. 366). And he appeals to Romans 13:1–2 and 1 Peter 2:13–14 as proof of the divinely ordained power of secular rulers, as well as to a range of texts as justifying their use of capital punishment: Genesis 4:14–15; 9:6; Exodus 21:14; 21:23–31; Matthew 26:52; Luke 3:14, and again 1 Peter 2:14.

So far, so good: but Luther is aware of other texts which seem to contradict this. Exodus 21:23–25 says: "If any harm follows, then you shall give life for life, eye for eye, tooth for tooth, hand for hand, foot for foot, burn for burn, wound for wound, stripe for stripe." The same text is cited and apparently set aside by Jesus in the Sermon on the Mount (Matthew 5:38–39): "You have heard that it was said, 'An eye for an eye and a tooth for a tooth.' But I say to you, Do not resist one who is evil. But if any one strikes you on the right cheek, turn to him the other also." How can such contrasting statements be reconciled? Earlier exegetes had attempted to do so by distinguishing precepts for ordinary Christians from counsels of perfection, intended only for advanced or perfect Christians. Luther resists such a move, for it would undermine the literal sense of what he understands as Jesus's commandment in Matthew 5:38–39. Jesus is certainly commanding people not to resist evil, but which people?

Luther's attempt to resolve the contradiction depends on the fateful distinction between two "kingdoms": "We must divide all the children of Adam into two classes: the first belong to the kingdom of God, the second to the kingdom of the world" (Dillenberger, p. 368). Jesus's commands are directed to Christians and are to be obeyed literally by them: they should not pursue their rights even where they might expect the assistance of the courts. Such people "need no secular sword or law." On the other hand, the ruler has a duty to restrain the wicked and to assist those who are wronged to find redress. "The law is not given for the righteous, but for the unrighteous" (1 Timothy 1:9). The two kingdoms "must be sharply distinguished, and both be permitted to remain: the one to produce piety, the other to bring about external peace and prevent evil deeds; neither is sufficient in the world without the other" (Dillenberger, p. 371).

This doctrine (which is not without its analogues in Augustine's contrast between the city of God and the earthly city) had an immense influence on the shaping of modern Europe. It established clearly distinguished spheres of influence for church and state which made for an easy coexistence between the two. This often went hand in hand with an alliance of the two which was all too convenient for both. The church lent its ideological support to the state; the state undergirded the authority of the church with its secular power; neither interfered in the other's affairs. In Germany this alliance of "throne and altar" allowed many Lutherans to accept Nazi rule during the Third Reich. "German Christians" formed an alliance with National Socialism. For those who rejected Nazi rule, however, this doctrine posed difficulties which were not easily overcome. To what extent could they—indeed should they—not merely interfere in the workings of the state, but actively work for the overthrow of a tyrannical regime? The

Lutheran theologian Dietrich Bonhoeffer was among those involved in the unsuccessful bomb plot against Hitler and paid for it with his life.

The attractions to Luther of such a separation are clear. It provided a clear theological position with which to resist secular interference in matters of faith. If Catholic rulers sought to impose the spiritual views of the papacy on his fellow evangelicals, Luther could condemn this as being outside their secular authority. But what if the ruler orders them to do something which is wrong in the secular sphere?

> Are his people bound to follow him then? I answer, No for it is no one's duty to do wrong; we ought to obey God Who desires the right, rather than men (Acts 5:29). How is it, when the subjects do not know whether the prince is in the right or not? I answer, As long as they cannot know, nor find out by any possible means, they may obey without peril to their souls.
>
> *Dillenberger, p. 399*

The Lutheran theologian and pastor Dietrich Bonhoeffer (1906–45) was hanged at the Flossenbürg concentration camp for his involvement in a plot to assassinate Hitler. Bonhoeffer's *The Cost of Discipleship* was a study of the Sermon on the Mount; it attacked the notion of "cheap grace," arguing that grace is costly and makes demands on those who receive it.

It does not require much imagination to see how such a statement can inspire both courageous resistance (of which Luther provided a powerful example) and provide the basis for compromise and ideological repression. Those who did not want to run the risks of opposing the will of the princes could invoke the principle of sufficient ignorance; the ruler in turn could appeal to the doctrine of original sin to claim that sin so clouded the minds of his subjects that they could in principle never know whether he was in the right or wrong. One of the Reimarus Fragments published by Lessing (see chapter 5) is entitled "Of the Denunciation of Reason from the Pulpit"; it attacks precisely this combination of autocratic rule with a theological denigration of reason, on grounds partly scriptural and partly rational. Nevertheless, such was the power of the alliance between church and state in the middle of the eighteenth century that Reimarus was unwilling to publish the manuscript himself. He kept it safely shut away, lest he himself be imprisoned and his family disgraced.

Allegiance to the State: Oaths and Arms-Bearing

Not all the Reformers were willing to make the clear separation between the worldly and the spiritual kingdoms that Luther made. The Anabaptists and others in the Radical Reformation tradition believed that Jesus's commands in the Sermon on the Mount (Matthew 5–7), particularly in those passages which oppose sayings from the Law with sayings of Jesus (the "antitheses"—Matthew 5:21–48), were to be taken as the guide for all human society. They argued that the old law had been superseded and that Jesus had come to announce a new law which would create a more just society. They put this view into practice quite straightforwardly, avoided ostentatious clothing and wealth, refused to swear oaths in court, to bear arms or to defend themselves. The citizens of St. Gallen in Switzerland pulled down the city gates, preferring to trust to God for their defense. If many found their ways strange and difficult, they could reply:

> Whoever finds God's command difficult, does not love God and does not know him, how good he is . . . God's covenant and the yoke of his son is heavy only to those who have not carried it . . . The more the elect works in God's vineyard, the less he tires; even the work is rest for him in God.
>
> *Hans Denck, quoted in Luz, p. 55*

This simple trust in the goodness of God's law and willingness to put it literally into practice was combined with a missionary zeal. Those who found the administration of oaths and the power of the sword to be a necessary means of maintaining law and order saw in these ardent advocates of an evangelical ethic a dire threat to civil stability and dealt with them fiercely. However, this rarely dampened their zeal.

One of the most interesting examples of such attempts to live out the teachings of the Sermon on the Mount in civil society is provided by the Quakers in Pennsylvania. Unlike Luther, they did not "divide the children of Adam into two classes," those of the kingdom of God and those of the kingdom of the world, but believed "that every man was enlightened by the divine Light of Christ," as George Fox had taught on the basis of his own experience of religious illumination and of John 1:9. There could therefore be no question—in theory at least—of two kinds of laws, one for Christians and one for the children of the world. Moreover, like the Anabaptists, they interpreted the commandments of the Sermon of the Mount literally and so refused to bear arms or to swear oaths.

Fox's position on oaths was clear: "Take heed of giving people oaths to swear, for Christ our Lord and master saith, 'Swear not at all; but let your communication be yea, yea, and nay, nay: for whatsoever is more than these cometh of evil.'" What gave truth to all and made them testify to it was the "light in every man"; oaths and swearing were but "idle words" for which men would answer on judgment day. The Old Testament rules for swearing oaths were specifically for the Jews and could not stand against the words of Jesus and James, who had forbidden all swearing. Fox had been brought to court in 1656 for advocating such views, but by 1689 Quakers were permitted to make a simple affirmation "in the presence of Almighty God" and at the same time excluded from giving evidence in criminal cases, serving as jurors, and holding public office.

In 1682 the colony of Pennsylvania was founded under the leadership of William Penn. In the same year a law was enacted that people should give witness by "solemnly promising to speak the truth, the whole

George Fox (1624–91) was the founder of the Religious Society of Friends, or Quakers—committed Christian pacifists who refuse to bear arms or swear oaths. Such practices receive strong support from the Sermon on the Mount.

truth and nothing but the truth." But there were problems. In the first place, the colony was still an English colony and conflict with English law was possible. Secondly, the colony attracted Irish and German settlers, who were uneasy with witnesses and jurors who would not take traditional oaths. After many difficulties a compromise was reached. The Crown agreed that Quakers themselves might make the affirmation in criminal cases and as officeholders without any reference to God, but it still insisted that others should take oaths and therefore that oaths should be administered to them by the appropriate officials. This had the effect of excluding Quakers from certain public offices, most significantly those of magistrates and judges.

More serious tests were to come over the question of arms-bearing, as Quakers were committed to pacifism. George Fox had refused to fight for the commonwealth against Charles Stuart. His position was firmly based on biblical texts:

> We are peaceable, and seek the peace, good, and welfare of all . . .
> For Christ said, "His Kingdom was not of this world, if it were his servants would fight." There he bid Peter, "put up his sword; for," said he, "he that taketh the sword shall perish by the sword." Here is the faith and patience of the saints, to bear and suffer all things, knowing vengeance is the Lord's, and he will repay to them that hurt his people and wrong the innocent; therefore cannot we avenge but suffer for his name's sake.
>
> *Boorstin, pp. 48–49*

While to the Quakers it might seem that they had escaped from England to a land where they would be free to pursue a peaceable way of life, free from the military and political ambitions of the British Crown, its status as a colony made this impossible. Thus they were involved in a series of wars against the French and the Spanish, but largely protected from the King's enemies by the colonies to the north and the south. In due course, however, war and attacks from the Indians who were being squeezed by the warring colonists, came to Pennsylvania. In 1755 settlers on the western frontier suffered terribly at the hands of the Indians and Franklin, then the leader of a compromise party in the Assembly, mobilized opinion in favor of raising the necessary military forces to defend the colony. In 1756 the Governor and the council declared war on the Delaware and Shewanee Indians. The Quaker majority in the Pennsylvania Assembly resigned.

One has to be careful in drawing lessons from this story. The American historian Daniel Boorstin, on whom I have largely depended

Benjamin Franklin, depicted in this reproduction of a portrait by Joseph-Siffrède Duplessis (1725–1802), had first organized a volunteer militia in the Pennsylvania colony in 1747, in an effort to defend the colonists from French and Spanish privateers who were raiding towns along the Delaware River. Of the opposition Franklin faced from the Quakers, he wrote: "Should we entreat them to consider, if not as Friends, at least as legislators, that protection is as truly due from the government to the people."

for the above account, laments the Quakers' concern with the purity of their own motives and actions and clearly believes that, if only they had been willing to compromise in a measure, they might have been able both to hold on to power and to exert a greater influence on the subsequent development of society in the United States. This is by no means an unfair point: but does it quite meet the case? It is hard to know where one can compromise as a pacifist without ceasing to be true to one's principles. This was presumably what lay behind the messages of their fellow Quakers in England, who urged them not to waver. They were a peaceable people and if they should ever take up arms they would lose their identity and cease to make the kind of witness that they could. They had set out, after all, to build a society where such principles would be followed as public policy. However, their affairs were never exclusively in their own hands, as the controversies over oath-swearing make clear. What went on in Pennsylvania was caught up in British imperial ambitions; others who came to live in the colony might have rather different understandings of the way to deal with those who pillaged their settlements. In short, Quaker attempts to make their principles into public policy failed to take into account the need to balance different and inevitably conflicting principles. And so they became a marginal but prophetic group willing to testify with their lives to the atrocity of war and coercion. This may not lead to long-lasting polities, such as those which Luther's doctrines spawned. It may, however, precisely by refusing to abandon the claim that such principles should have a bearing on public life, have a continuing contribution to make, long after the attempt to make a sharp distinction between the ethics of the spiritual and the worldly kingdoms has been finally discredited.

Gender Politics

The histories we have just been considering were all concerned with attempts to translate the injunctions of the Gospels into guiding principles for civil society. The flaw with both Luther on the one hand and the Anabaptists and the Quakers on the other lay in the belief that such a process of translation could be relatively direct and straightforward, as if it were merely a question of translating from one language into another. But the attempt to turn sayings from the Gospels and Paul into social and political reality in the sixteenth and seventeenth/eighteenth centuries clearly required more than that. It needed to take much more note of the social conditions of the times: the power and conflicting interests of the German princes in the case of Luther (who did take account of this, though without recognizing the extent to which it shaped his reading of scripture) and the interference of the British Crown and its imperial ambitions in the case of the Quakers.

I want, finally, to look at a topic where there is much more controversy about the desirability of embodying the injunctions of the Bible into contemporary society: gender politics. This is an area in which many have a very clear awareness of the need both for a critical reading of scripture and for a critical and imaginative engagement between scripture and present-day reality.

In a word, there is much in the Bible which is undeniably patriarchal, which commands women to be submissive to men and which exalts maleness over femaleness. We noticed earlier the attitudes to women in the two creation narratives. The New Testament contains injunctions to women to be silent in church (1 Corinthians 14:34) and to wives to be submissive to their husbands in all things (Ephesians 5:21–33). Such sayings have been taken up and incorporated into the life of the churches over the centuries to the point where, with the rise of feminism, many women have felt that there is no longer any place for them in mainstream churches. Others, however, still believe that there are resources within the churches and the Bible which are liberating and can lead the church and society to embrace more egalitarian, less hierarchical forms of association. How do they proceed?

In the first instance, commentators like the American Old Testament scholar Phyllis Trible have worked, with great passion, to raise people's awareness of the oppressiveness of many of the biblical narratives. In her *Texts of Terror*, she brings out the terrifying nature of the way in which women are treated in some of them. In Judges 11, Jephthah vows to God that he will sacrifice the first person that he meets coming out of his house after his forthcoming battle, if he is successful. The fact that it is his daughter does not deter him from keeping his vow. And there is much more of this kind, some of which we considered when reviewing Margaret Atwood's *The Handmaid's Tale*.

Such a consciousness-raising exercise is necessary if the Bible is to be made use of at all in attempting to find alternatives to patriarchy. But what positive resources does it offer? Let me consider two rather different, though complementary, approaches to this question. Elisabeth Schüssler-Fiorenza, a New Testament scholar teaching in the United States, has sought in her work to rewrite the history of early Christianity to show the importance within it of egalitarian traditions stemming from Jesus. Jesus in his preaching of the kingdom proclaims that salvation is dawning. The reality of this new salvation is symbolized in his meals: "It is the festive table-sharing at a wedding-feast, and not the ascesis of the 'holy man,' that characterizes Jesus and his movement . . . Not the holiness of the elect, but the wholeness *of all* is the central vision of Jesus"

The Gospel accounts of Jesus's resurrection do not precisely agree as to who was present when Jesus arose from the dead, but in all four accounts it is women who discover the empty tomb. This fresco, painted by Fra Angelico for the convent of San Marco in Florence—where the artist, a Dominican friar, resided in the 1430s and 1440s—depicts the resurrected Christ with a group of women at the right and an angel at the left. Saint Dominic kneels in meditation at the far left.

(Schüssler-Fiorenza 1983, pp. 119, 121). All are included, "[w]omen as well as men, prostitutes as well as Pharisees." Jesus's vision is therefore opposed to patriarchy, to any attempt to divide the united community, to set one section against another. A key text for Schüssler-Fiorenza is Galatians 3:28: "There is neither Jew nor Greek, there is neither slave nor free, there is neither male nor female; for you are all one in Christ Jesus." But also important are the Gospel traditions which set aside the patriarchal family relationships in favor of the "discipleship of equals" of those who "do the will of God": they are the ones who are to be called "my brother, and sister, and mother" (Mark 3:35). Thus all titles and hierarchical distinctions are to be set aside: "And call no man your father on earth, for you have one Father, who is in heaven. Neither be called masters, for you have one master, the Christ" (Matthew 23:9–10) (Schüssler-Fiorenza 1993, pp. 176–77). Moreover, this egalitarian ethos is reflected in the history of the early Christian mission, where women played a full role together with men.

Such traditions were not uncontested, as indeed the New Testament writings themselves make clear. Within them one can discern a tendency to suppress evidence of the role of women in the earliest Christian communities and of the growing patriarchalization of the community in the second and third generations. Thus there is clear evidence within the Gospels of a "discipleship of equals," with women playing an important part in key events, remaining at the cross, being primary witnesses to the Resurrection (John 20:11–18). However Luke's Gospel, often thought of as being the most sympathetic to women, excludes women from the witnesses: the apostles alone see the risen Jesus. Whereas Paul in 1 Corinthians 15:5–8 has a wide list of those who can operate as authoritative witnesses to Jesus's death and resurrection (although even here there is no explicit mention of women), Luke gives no account of any resurrection appearance to women; instead he emphasizes the appearance to Peter. Schüssler-Fiorenza believes that this emphasis on Peter must "be situated within the early Christian discussion of whether Peter or Mary of Magdala qualifies as the first resurrection witness" (Schüssler-Fiorenza 1993, p. 164).

Schüssler-Fiorenza describes her work in *In Memory of Her* as a "feminist theological reconstruction of Christian origins." It is an attempt to recover a history of Christian origins which has been obscured, partly by patriarchal tendencies within the New Testament itself, partly by the subsequent historiography of the church. Such a reconstruction is theological in that it looks for the key theological vision of Jesus and the early Christians; it is feminist in that its critical reading of the New Testament texts is informed and impelled by the experience of "women's struggle for liberation from oppression" (Schüssler-Fiorenza 1983, p. 32). It treats the New Testament, or rather the picture of the church that it presents, not as a timeless archetype of the ideal form of church life, but as a prototype "which is critically open to the possibility of its own transformation" (p. 33).

Other feminist writers treat the Bible and its stories, images, and metaphors, alongside women's writing of all kinds, as imaginative resources for the refashioning of the church's traditions. Mary Grey, an English Catholic theologian, in *Beyond the Dark Night*, deploys a whole cluster of images in an attempt to conjure up the new form of the church which will emerge in and through its "dark night." In a chapter on journeying, she explores the "condensed symbol of exodus from oppression, wandering in the wilderness—while experiencing the presence of God in a way—and hoping for the Promised Land" (Grey, p. 48). Use of such symbols, of the "creative imagination is a key tool in journeying from alienated forms of Christian living." Images of the Exodus, which were so important an inspiration for liberation theology, no longer provide spiritual dynamism to those in former communist countries who are now themselves suffering in their new life within the capitalist fold. "The vision of the socialist Utopia had vanished, and what remained were the seductive arms of capitalism. Wandering in the wilderness without vision summed up their situation symbolically" (Grey p. 48). In such situations, images of exile may exert a more powerful attraction. What Mary Grey advocates is not exodus from the church, but the refocusing of symbols of exodus as symbols of exodus from "alienated relationships."

> A sacramental life which alienates large categories of believers from the table of the Eucharist is in danger of being alienated sacramental life . . . A theology of sexuality which condemns to the status of deviants . . . a large proportion of human beings is alienated sexuality. Understandings of power, priesthood, and authority which reduce the pilgrim people to disempowerment and passivity are alienated understandings.
>
> *Grey, p. 50*

Here biblical imagery is contextualized: the images and symbolism of the Bible are drawn on freely in a search for wholeness and inclusion in the face of alienating forces in church and community, which threaten to stifle and break human relationships. The Bible is not appealed to as a set of norms, but drawn on, freely and selectively, as a resource of imagery which can give shape and form to people's life experiences.

The Bible as Political Authority

This has been a necessarily partial survey of the uses of the Bible in politics. It would have been possible to include many other issues in public

The Bible occupies a central position, symbolic of its status as a political authority, in this artistic interpretation of Abraham Lincoln writing the Emancipation Proclamation. The print, based on a painting by David Gilmour Blythe (1815–65), depicts Lincoln, whose left hand rests on a Bible that in turn rests on a copy of the Constitution, in his study along with other symbolic objects, including busts of two previous presidents and the scales of Justice.

policy: welfare, slavery, economics, genetics, medicine, and so on. Given the enormous status and authority of the Bible in Europe throughout most of the last two thousand years, this is hardly surprising. Politicians would hardly be politicians if they were to ignore potential sources of ideological support—or indeed opposition.

Even in such a survey it is difficult not to be struck by the conflicting ways in which the Bible has been used. Luther and the mainstream Reformers used it to justify the power of the sword and to draw a clear line between the laws which were to govern secular society and the teaching of the Sermon on the Mount which was intended only for Christians. Those who on the other hand insisted that Jesus's teachings should be put into practice in the life of the state had then to face the practical difficulties of embodying statements of great generality in institutions and legislation for very particular communities facing quite specific situations and dangers. Both sides of this debate, however, were agreed in seeing the Bible as a book with a coherent consistent message for the church and society, however much they might disagree about the nature of that message. The feminist critics we have looked at are much clearer that there is plenty in the Bible which is unacceptable and that the real struggle is to discern those elements which could provide resources in the search for a new church and a new society. Here the process of discernment is ultimately to be governed by the experience of women's struggles. But equally, different strategies can be devised for separating the more creative resources out from the rest. For some, historical criticism could enable them to discern elements in the tradition almost obscured by subsequent ideological bias. For others, it is the recontextualizing of biblical imagery and symbolism which can assist the imaginative leap whereby new forms of life and community can emerge out of the biblical traditions. To return to earlier discussions, we may see at work here two rather different conceptions of the canon. For the first, the canon is still seen as normative, although it is a norm which has first to be established by historical discernment of the truly binding elements within the texts. For the latter, the canonical authority of the Bible is first and foremost formative: it provides the tools and imagery which can both enslave and liberate. Discernment is just as necessary: however, the test is practical rather than historical.

NINE

Conclusion

●

I HOPE THIS BRIEF SURVEY OF THE BIBLE and its uses has shown something of the richness of the ways in which it has been read and appropriated. It has inspired some of the great monuments of human thought, literature, and art; it has equally fuelled some of the worst excesses of human savagery, self-interest, and narrow-mindedness. It has inspired men and women to acts of great service and courage, to fight for liberation and human development; and it has provided the ideological fuel for societies which have enslaved their fellow human beings and reduced them to abject poverty. It has been at the root of the great revivals of Christianity, most recently in its remarkable growth in Africa and Asia. It has, perhaps above all, provided a source of religious

In this detail from Leonardo da Vinci's *Annunciation* (painted 1472–75, now in the Uffizi Gallery in Florence), the Virgin Mary's hand holds her place in a Bible, which—according to Christian iconographic tradition—she had been reading just as the angel Gabriel arrived to announce that she would be bearing the Christ child.

and moral norms which have enabled communities to hold together, to care for, and to protect one another; yet precisely this strong sense of belonging has in turn fueled ethnic, racial, and international tension and conflict.

It has, that is to say, been the source of great truth, goodness, and beauty at the same time as it has inspired lies, wickedness, and ugliness. What it has not produced is a uniform manner of its reading and interpretation. The reason for this is simple: texts have no control over the way they are read. "Texts," wrote Robert Morgan, "like dead men, have no rights" (Morgan, p. 7). It is the reader or communities of readers who produce the readings. And the diversity of readings produced is in proportion to the diversity of reading communities.

Such diversity should not, however, be attributed solely to the diversity of readers. The sheer richness of material in the Bible, the complexity of the processes whereby its books came to be written, the profusion of metaphor, of poetry, of narrative and discourse, would hardly lead us to expect that this collection of books would receive a single uncontroversial reading. At all times and in all places its many readers have had plenty to choose from, every opportunity to emphasize different aspects.

This diversity of material within the Bible has of course been a source of concern for leaders of religious communities, who have seen in their sacred writings a source of religious and moral norms, of revealed truth. The very process of canonization, of establishing an agreed list of books which are recognized as authoritative and excluding others which are not, is part of an attempt to limit diversity and deviance of belief within the community. Within Christianity, the creation of a second canon of New Testament scripture represents a further attempt to determine and limit the ways in which scripture is read: the Old is to be read through the lens of the New; but equally the New will receive a particular set of meanings from being linked with the Old.

Furthermore, once the boundaries of the canon are set, the books within it can never be read in quite the same way again, at least within those communities which accept them as canonical. For they have now become part of an authoritative corpus: they have been declared to be the word of God and there must then be limits to the diversity of viewpoint which can be tolerated among them. Once texts are canonized, the believers' expectations of them soar. Readers have to read them according to a "principle of charity" whereby they are read not only in such a way as to make sense (even though parts of them may appear obscure and incomprehensible), but also in such a way as to explain apparent or real contradictions and to rework the meaning of passages that may otherwise seem to contradict the teachings of the authorizing body.

But the fact is that canonization of sacred writings is a very rough tool for dealing with religious deviance. The sheer diversity of Protestant churches, all of which recognize the same canon, is ample proof of this. If there is to be a measure of consistency in scriptural interpretation within a given community and hence a measure of stability within that community, further strategies will be needed. This may be achieved in different ways. In the first place, access to the sacred books may be restricted. Only readers who have the required skills and qualifications for interpreting them in ways which will ensure uniformity and continuity of interpretation will be admitted. Within Judaism, this role falls to the scholar/rabbi. Within Christianity, it falls to the clergy, acting under the authority of the bishops or other kinds of church leaders.

The task of these interpreters is partly to lay down the rules of interpretation, partly to construe the texts in such a way that they do indeed offer a reading which is self-consistent and consistent with the norms of the community. With a collection of sacred texts as diverse as those contained in the Bible this will entail not only devising strategies for accommodating passages whose most evident sense is in flagrant contradiction to the central beliefs of the community; it will also entail setting emphases—highlighting certain texts and relegating others to relative insignificance. Crucially, it will entail devising techniques, such as allegory, whereby meanings can be imparted to texts whose literal sense is either unedifying or simply in conflict with the rule of faith of the community. The history of interpretation of the Bible provides rich pickings for those who look for examples of interpretative dexterity and imagination.

Within such rules and interpretative practices, there is then room for a controlled diversity of reading. Interpreters can relate the texts to the experience of their readers and indeed, as we have seen, allow such experience to affect their retelling of the text. There is room for debate and controversy, and there is the stuff of real division. The medieval church managed to contain diversity of interpretation by a mixture of high-level control—theological and political—and permitted diversity of theologies, forms of life, and religious orders. It also relied on ruthless suppression or marginalization of those whom it deemed deviants, such as Jews, Cathars, and Hussites. It certainly produced its share of deviants, among them the Augustinian friar who would destroy its unity, Martin Luther.

Luther's attack on the sacramental order of the church, with its clerical monopoly on the dispensing of grace, was altogether an attack

Martin Luther's translation of the Bible into German, first published in 1534, was one of the first efforts to make the Bible accessible to a readership outside the clergy. This title page comes from a 1554 edition published by the German printer Michael Lotter.

from within. It was based on his interpretation of the Pauline texts about justification by faith. It relied on a strictly grammatical reading of these texts, something which was entirely permissible under the existing rules and practices of interpretation in the late medieval church. Luther himself was an accredited teacher of the Bible. In normal circumstances such anomalous behavior could have been dealt with internally too. A number of factors made his attack fatal, not the least of which was the invention of the printing press, which enabled his views to be rapidly and widely disseminated. At the same time his (and others') translations of the Bible into the vernacular provided wide popular access to the texts which till then had been largely the preserve of the clergy. The clerical monopoly was broken; from now on every man and woman could be their own interpreter.

· · · · ·

The Protestant principle that everyone could be his or her own interpreter of Scripture (as opposed to the Catholic view that the tradition of the church as established in the church councils was the true interpreter of Scripture) was pilloried by a sixteenth-century Catholic scholar in the following terms:

> This Biblicist is a single person. The fathers of the council can be any number. This Biblicist is a sheep . . . the fathers of the council are pastors and bishops. This Biblicist prays by himself. The fathers of the council pray for all who are present at the council, indeed for the whole Christian world . . . This Biblicist may be an uneducated woman. They . . . are the most learned men in the Christian world.
>
> *Valerianus Magni,* De acatholicorum credendi regula iudicium *(An assessment of the rule of believing of non-Catholics), in Scholder, p. 18*

· · · · ·

The subsequent explosion of new readings of the Bible, of new forms of religious devotion and ways of life, is hardly adequately described as a reformation. The Reformers may indeed have seen it in just those terms: returning to the true form of the church as revealed in scripture to those who would read and follow its plain, literal sense. In practice what happened was much more like the opening of Pandora's box: once the winds were out, there was no way of putting them back. Older readings of scripture would continue to have their place alongside a whole variety of new ones. New religious communities would spring up all over Europe and from there spread out all over the globe. It was a time of great renewal and life, which in turn provoked fierce conflict and recrimination. Nearly a third of the population of Europe died in the conflagration of the religious wars in the first half of the sixteenth century. Yet even beyond such conflict the Bible has continued to provide communities with a basis for living and has, as we have seen, taken root in communities all over the globe, even among peoples who have experienced abuse in its name. Diversity of readings, it seems, is here to stay.

Of course, there are still those who believe that such developments can be reversed. There are those who believe that their community still has the key to the proper interpretation of scripture, whether this be in the form of some infallible teaching office, of some theological rule or confession which can act as a test of true readings of the texts, or indeed of a historical method which can deliver the original, single meaning of the text.

The difficulty with theological keys is this: either they are so specific, so closely tied to one particular community, that they are of little use in resolving disputes between communities; or they are so general, framed so widely, that they fail to address points of specific difference. If, for example, a particular church wishes to uphold one of the Reformation confessions of faith as its "subordinate standard of faith," this may indeed enable it to adjudicate in internal disputes about the proper interpretation of scripture: it will not, however, enable the resolution of interdenominational differences, where it is precisely the difference between the various confessions of faith which is at issue. If on the other hand, one were to propose some much more general principle of interpretation, say that all interpretations should be broadly Trinitarian in scope, this would generate only a relatively weak set of rules whereby to adjudicate between different Christian interpretations. It would of course also be too specifically Christian to be of use in cases of interfaith disagreement.

The alternative to such an approach is to try and find some apparently neutral method of interpretation to which all can appeal, regardless of cultural stance. Here the historical critical method has seemed to many to be a most promising candidate. Just as Luther asked "what the Apostle wanted" as a way to resolve disputes over the meaning of a text in Romans, so one might seek to resolve other disputes by searching for the original meaning intended by the author. There are a number of problems with this proposal. In the first place, it is doubtful whether authorial intention will do the job that it is asked to. Are authors' intentions as clear as all that? T. S. Eliot once replied when asked if an interpretation of his poetry corresponded to what he had meant: "What I meant is what I wrote." Secondly, and perhaps more problematically, historians are inevitably influenced by their own point of view. This is partly a matter of their place within a particular tradition of reading, with its own body of knowledge, cultural beliefs, and standpoints, and partly a matter of their own tastes, preferences, and prejudices, formed in a broader cultural context. All of this will shape their judgments, with the result that historians

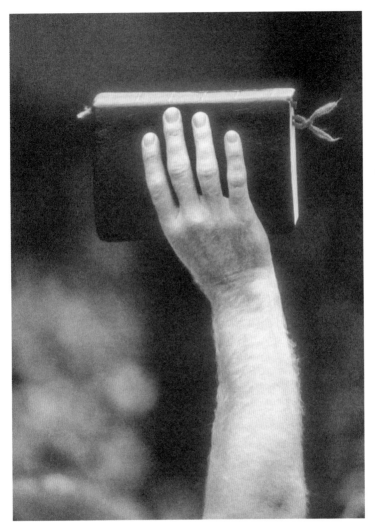

Interpretations of the Bible often differ among various communities of faith, each relying on its own moral convictions and cultural experience as a guide. This photograph of a hand raising a Bible was taken at a Christian evangelical meeting in Tulsa, Oklahoma.

will inevitably produce a plurality of readings. One would have to be blind as a historian to the diversity of historical readings (produced by eminent scholars) not to realize the truth of this. It does not mean that appeal to historical arguments may never be of use; nor does it mean that we learn nothing about the texts from such enquiries. It does mean that we will be most unlikely to resolve many disputes by recourse to such a line of argument.

So perhaps readers of the Bible will have to live with the fact that it has a rich potential for generating different meanings. Maybe, indeed, they should come to see this not simply as a problem with the Bible, but also as part of its very strength. This has serious consequences. It means firstly that the normative function of the Bible for any community is significantly weakened. If the Bible is recognized as essentially capable of many meanings, its use as a code of conduct or indeed as a rule of faith will be limited. But has this not always been the case? The fact that Jews will appeal to the Talmudim for rulings on matters of practice and belief and that Christians have appealed to some rule of faith or to the canons of the ecumenical councils to regulate their affairs suggests clearly enough that in practice it has always been accepted that the Bible was either too rich or too diverse or too vague to do the job of a Code Napoleon.

On the other hand, recognizing the Bible's potential for generating different meanings does not mean that its formative function is weakened in the same way. The whole point of our argument has been to show how powerful the influence of the Bible has been in the formation of a whole range of communities. Such power is not without its dangers. It has generated some deeply oppressive settler communities, just as it has produced reformers, liberationist politicians, and peacemakers.

What it certainly means is that we have to learn to read the Bible more critically. We have to become better attuned to the different voices within the biblical texts. Equally we also need to be aware of the different kinds of uses to which the Bible may be put and to learn to discriminate among them.

In these tasks the various approaches that we have considered all have their role to play. The historian of religion precisely by discerning different tendencies and influences in the texts may help us to be more aware of its complexity. Schüssler-Fiorenza's analysis of the patriarchal tendencies in Luke alerts us to the way that certain traditions have been marginalized in the Bible—and indeed in subsequent readings of the Bible—in ways which enable us to hear voices which we might otherwise have missed. Similarly, Mary Grey's imaginative use of wilderness motifs may serve to inspire people to live through the toils of a church emerging from patriarchy and to discover forms of communal living which are more integrative, more humane.

Again, readers will be guided by the rules and interpretative practices of the communities to which they belong. Those within Christian communities will be deeply influenced by the form(s) of the Christian canon. Its setting of the New Testament alongside the Old creates, as we saw in Desmond Tutu's reading of the Naboth story, a powerful theological framework within which to read the texts.

Even so, readers will have to judge for themselves between the different interpretations which any such approach makes possible. In this they will in a sense be thrown back on their own moral resources. But it is not simply a matter of individuals sitting in judgment over the biblical texts: the process of reading is more complex. In the first place, readers are rarely alone: they belong to communities which have been shaped by the text and which have in turn schooled their own moral senses. Thus the thoughtful reader is always engaged in a process of testing inherited moral senses against the texts and, as we have seen in so many cases, against his own experience. Will it stretch or will it break? Are there other senses among the readings which are possible from a particular perspective which will lead out of seeming impasses, which can bring renewal to traditions which are drying up or, worse, leading to oppression and self-deception?

Moreover, in this process readers are not simply dependent upon their own inherited values. As they learn to discriminate between the different voices in the texts, between different readings and constructions of the text, their moral and religious imagination and judgment is informed and sharpened. Where such discriminating and attentive reading occurs, communal traditions will be nourished and kept alive; where they are absent or marginalized, the tradition will wither. Even then, not all may be lost: from time to time there emerge moral and prophetic figures in whom the ideas and images of the texts have taken deep root, who may renew their inherited traditions or else generate new communities of their own.

One of the remarkable features of the Bible which we have noticed too little is its age. Its earliest material is some three thousand years old; most of it is two thousand years old and the New Testament only just slightly younger. From time to time people cast doubt on the ability of such ancient texts to speak to people so far removed in time. Certainly if the texts were limited only to the meaning which they carried (and were intended to carry) for their first hearers, we might well wonder whether they would have any future in an age so different as ours. But their history demonstrates that their stories, images, metaphors, and moral and religious concepts have shaped and continue to shape the experience and understanding of peoples of great diversity. Recent history in Africa and Asia suggests that there is no diminishing of this power. What are required are discriminating readers, alert to its life-giving potential, on their guard against its darker tones.

REFERENCES AND
FURTHER READING

•

Unless stated otherwise in the text, biblical references are taken from the Revised Standard Version.

CHAPTER 1

Boyarin, Daniel. *A Radical Jew: Paul and the Politics of Identity.* Berkeley: University of California Press, 1994).
Ruthven, Malise. *The Divine Supermarket: Shopping for God in America.* London: Vintage, 1991.

CHAPTER 2

A good introduction to the history of the formation of the books of the Bible is to be found in the relevant articles in the new *Anchor Bible Dictionary* (Doubleday, New York: 1992). The article on Torah (Pentateuch), vol. 6, pp. 605–22, by Richard Friedman is particularly helpful. For a good introduction to the Synoptic Gospels, see either Graham Stanton, *The Gospels and Jesus* (Oxford University Press, Oxford: 1989), or E. P. Sanders and Margaret Davies, *Studying the Synoptic Gospels* (SCM Press,

London: 1989). For a general introduction to Paul and his writings, see E. P. Sanders, *Paul* (Oxford University Press, Oxford: 1991).

CHAPTER 3

The articles on "Canon" by James A. Sanders and Harry Y. Gamble in the *Anchor Bible Dictionary*, vol. 1, pp. 837–61, are very useful. John Barton has made a particular study of the origin of the canon and of the nature of its authority: see especially his *People of the Book? The Authority of the Bible in Christianity* (SPCK, London: 1988); *Making the Christian Bible* (Darton, Longman, and Todd, London: 1997); and *The Spirit and the Letter: Studies in the Biblical Canon* (SPCK, London: 1997). See too James A. Sanders, *From Sacred Story to Sacred Text* (Fortress Press, Philadelphia: 1987); Hans von Campenhausen, *The Formation of the Christian Bible* (Fortress Press, Philadelphia: 1972). Moshe Halberthal, *People of the Book: Canon, Meaning, and Authority* (Harvard University Press, Cambridge, MA: 1997), provides a fascinating discussion of different kinds of canonical authority and the effect canonization has on the way texts are read.

CHAPTER 4

The text of the Book of Jubilees is to be found in J. Charlesworth (ed.), *The Old Testament Pseudepigrapha* (Darton, Longman, and Todd, London 1985), vol. 2, pp. 35–142. Philo's *De Abrahamo* can be found in the Loeb Classical Library, Philo vol. 6 (Harvard University Press, Cambridge, MA: 1984), pp. 2–135. Shalom Spiegel, *The Last Trial: On the Legends and Lore of the Command to Abraham to Offer Isaac as a Sacrifice: The Akedah* (Jewish Lights Publishing, Woodstock, VT: 1993), provides a rich discussion of Jewish retellings of the story, together with the full text of Rabbi Ephraim ben Jacob of Bonn's poem. Søren Kierkegaard's discussion is in *Fear and Trembling* (ed. and trans. H. V. and E. H. Hong, Princeton University Press, Princeton, NJ: 1983). The Goldin quotation is from the Introduction of Shalom Spiegel, *The Last Trial*.

CHAPTER 5

Quite the best treatment of the rise of biblical criticism is to be found in Klaus Scholder's *The Birth of Modern Critical Theology: Origins and Problems of Biblical Criticism in the Seventeenth Century* (SCM Press, London: 1990). John Dillenberger's *Martin Luther: Selections from His Writings* (Doubleday, New York: 1961) gives a useful selection. Luther's discussion of his attempts to understand Romans 1:17 is to be found in *The Preface to the Latin Writings* of 1545. Leslie Stephen's *History of English Thought in the Eighteenth Century* (Rupert Hart-Davis, London: 1962), 2 vols, is a classic treatment of English Deism. *Reimarus: Fragments* (ed. C. H. Talbert) gives a translation of only some of the sections of Reimarus's Apology which Lessing published. Henry Chadwick (ed.), *Lessing's Theological Writings: Selections in Translation* (A & C Black, London: 1956), gives some of the important Lessing texts. Albert Schweitzer, *The Quest for the Historical Jesus: A Critical Study of Its Progress from Reimarus to Wrede* (A & C Black, London: 1910, 2nd edn., 1936), is the most lasting literary work of this theologian, musicologist, organist, missionary doctor, and philosopher of religion.

CHAPTER 6

An excellent guide to the use of the Bible in the colonial period is provided by Michael Prior, CM, *The Bible and Colonialism: A Moral Critique* (Sheffield Academic Press, Sheffield: 1997). I have quoted from the following works cited by Prior: Pablo Richard, "1492: The Violence of God and the Future of Christianity," in Leonardo Boff and Virgil Elizondo (eds), *1492–1992: The Voice of the Victims, Concilium*, 1990, p. 6 (SCM Press, London: 1990), pp. 59–67; Maximiliano Salinas, "The Voices of Those Who Speak Up for the Victims" *Concilium*, 1990 (SCM Press, London: 1990), pp. 101–9. Gustavo Gutierrez, *A Theology of Liberation* (SCM Press, London: 1971), is one of the classics of Liberation Theology. His later *The God of Life* (SCM Press, London: 1991) is in the form of a biblical meditation. G. Pixley, *On Exodus: A Liberation Perspective* (Orbis, Maryknoll, NY: 1983), takes up the work of Norman Gottwald, *The Tribes of Yahweh: A Sociology of Religion of Liberated Israel, 1250–1050 BCE* (SCM Press, London: 1979). Desmond Tutu, *Hope and Suffering* (Collins, London: 1984), brings together a collection of Tutu's sermons and speeches delivered during the apartheid era. Musa W. Dube, "Readings of *Semoya*: Botswana Women's Interpretation of Matt. 15:21–28," in Gerald West and Musa W. Dube (eds), *"Reading With": An Exploration of the Interface between Critical and Ordinary Readings of the Bible: African Overtures, Semeia 73* (Scholars Press, Atlanta, GA: 1996), is part of a volume of essays exploring African readings of the Bible.

CHAPTER 7

Northrop Frye, *The Great Code: The Bible and Literature* (Harcourt Brace Jovanovich, New York: 1981), was one of the foundational works in the study of the influence of the Bible on European literature. For a general introduction to Bach's music, see Malcolm Boyd, *Bach* (Oxford University Press, Oxford 1990). Owen's poems are most easily available in C. Day Lewis (ed.), *The Collected Poems of Wilfred Owen* (Chatto & Windus, London: 1977). Mieke Bal, *Reading "Rembrandt": Beyond the Word-Image Opposition* (Cambridge University Press, Cambridge: 1992), gives a fascinating account of Rembrandt as an interpreter of the Bible. Margaret Atwood, *The Handmaid's Tale* (Virago Press, London: 1987), is discussed in David Jasper and Stephen Prickett (eds), *The Bible and Literature: A Reader* (Blackwell, Oxford: 1999).

CHAPTER 8

Quotations from Luther are taken from Dillenberger (see references to chapter 5). Ulrich Luz, "Die Bergpredigt im Spiegel ihrer Wirkungsge-schichte," in Jürgen Moltmann (ed.), *Nachfolge und Bergpredigt* (Kaiser Verlag, Munich: 1981), pp. 31–72. Daniel J. Boorstin, *The Americans: The Colonial Experience* (Vintage Books, New York: 1958), pp. 33–69, gives a critical view of Quaker history in Pennsylvania. The classic Quaker text is to be found in Rufus M. Jones (ed.), *The Journal of George Fox* (Friends United Press, Richmond, IN: 1976). Elisabeth Schüssler-Fiorenza, *In Memory of Her: A Feminist Theological Reconstruction of Christian Origins* (Crossroad, New York: 1983), uses historical research into the New Testament to uncover the more liberative strands which lie behind it. The importance of this for the understanding of the church is drawn out in her *Discipleship of Equals: A Critical Feminist Ekklesia-logy of Liberation* (SCM Press, London: 1993). Mary Grey, *Beyond the Dark Night: A Way Forward for the Church* (Cassell, London: 1997), looks for ways out of the present dilemma of the Catholic Church.

CHAPTER 9

Robert Morgan with John Barton, *Biblical Interpretation* (Oxford University Press, Oxford: 1988).

INDEX OF
BIBLICAL REFERENCES

•

OLD TESTAMENT

New Testament

Apocrypha and Pseudepigrapha

INDEX

•

Note: Page numbers in *italics* include illustrations, photographs/captions, and tables.

PICTURE CREDITS

•

89: Andrea Mantegna 036.jpg/Source: The Yorck Project: *10.000 Meisterwerke der Malerei*. DVD-ROM, 2002. ISBN 3936122202. Distributed by DIRECT-MEDIA Publishing GmbH; 91: ReuternAbraham.jpg/Source: http://www.picture.art-catalog.ru/artist.php?id_artist=252/User: The Deceiver; 92: Kreuzwegstationen Bamberger Dom.jpg/Author: Immanuel Giel; 98: Wenceslas Hollar - The Augsburg Confession (State 2).jpg/Source: University of Toronto Wenceslaus Hollar Digital Collection/User: Dcoetzee; 102: Luther46c.jpg/User: CTSWyneken; 108: Philipp-Melanchthon-1532.jpg/User: Torsten Schleese; 111l: Hermann Samuel Reimarus.jpg/Source: Almut Spalding, *Elise Reimarus (1735–1805): The Muse of Hamburg* (Würzburg: Königshausen & Neumann, 2005)/Painter: Gerloff Hiddinga/User: Paulae; 111r: Gotthold Ephraim Lessing Kunstsammlung Uni Leipzig.jpg/Source: http://www.uni-leipzig.de/cumpraxi/studium.html/Painter: Anton Graff/Upload by de: Benutzer/ALE!; 118: Benin baptism.jpg/Author: Ferdinand Reus; 135: Folio 164r - The Canaanite Woman. jpg/User: Petrusbarbygere; 140: Onthemorningthomas2.jpg/Source: http://freechristimages.org/biblestories/shepherds_in_the_field.htm/User: Lithoderm; 142: 6-406 Now night her course began.jpg/User: Captaincaptions; 150: Wilfred Owen.png/User: Ranveig; 153: Lastjudgement.jpg/Source: http://mv.vatican.va/3_EN/pages/x-Schede/CSNs/CSNs_G_Giud_big.html/User: FranksValli; 154: Giotto di Bondone 009.jpg/Source: The Yorck Project: *10.000 Meisterwerke der Malerei*. DVD-ROM, 2002. ISBN 3936122202. Distributed by DIRECTMEDIA Publishing GmbH; 157: Rembrandt Harmensz. van Rijn 054.jpg/Source: The Yorck Project: *10.000 Meisterwerke der Malerei*. DVD-ROM, 2002. ISBN 3936122202. Distributed by DIRECTMEDIA Publishing GmbH; 162: Andrea Mantegna 099.jpg/Source: The Yorck Project: *10.000 Meisterwerke der Malerei*. DVD-ROM, 2002. ISBN 3936122202. Distributed by DIRECTMEDIA Publishing GmbH; 168–69: Masaccio 004.jpg/Source: The Yorck Project: *10.000 Meisterwerke der Malerei*. DVD-ROM, 2002. ISBN 3936122202. Distributed by DIRECTMEDIA Publishing GmbH; 182: Fra Angelico 019.jpg/Source: The Yorck Project: *10.000 Meisterwerke der Malerei*. DVD-ROM, 2002. ISBN 3936122202. Distributed by DIRECTMEDIA Publishing GmbH; 190: Léonard de Vinci - Annonciation.jpg/Source: *Tout l'œuvre peint de Léonard de Vinci* (Paris: Flammarion, collection Les Classiques de l'art, 1968) ISBN 9782080102379/User: Oxxo; 195: BibelMagdeburg.jpg/Source: http://www.gwlb.de/sammlungen/sondersammlungen/bibeln/CIM89106aa.jpg/Upload by Concord

BRIEF INSIGHTS

•

A series of concise, engrossing, and enlightening books that explore
every subject under the sun with unique insight.

Available now or coming soon: